Mastering Azure Security

Safeguard your Azure workload with innovative cloud security measures

Mustafa Toroman

Tom Janetscheck

BIRMINGHAM—MUMBAI

Mastering Azure Security

Commissioning Editor: Vijin Boricha
Acquisition Editor: Shrilekha Inani
Senior Editor: Rahul Dsouza
Content Development Editor: Alokita Amanna
Technical Editor: Sarvesh Jaywant
Copy Editor: Safis Editing
Project Coordinator: Neil Dmello
Proofreader: Safis Editing
Indexer: Pratik Shirodkar
Production Designer: Aparna Bhagat

First published: May 2020

Production reference: 1060520

Published by Packt Publishing Ltd.
Livery Place
35 Livery Street
Birmingham

B3 2PB, UK.

ISBN 978-1-83921-899-6

www.packt.com

Contributors

About the authors

Mustafa Toroman is a program architect and lead system engineer with Authority Partners. With years of experience in designing and monitoring infrastructure solutions, lately, he focuses on designing new solutions in the cloud and migrating existing solutions to the cloud. He is very interested in DevOps processes, and he's also an Infrastructure-as-Code enthusiast. Mustafa has over 50 Microsoft certificates and has been an MCT for the last 8 years. He often speaks at international conferences about cloud technologies, and he was awarded the MVP for Microsoft Azure in 2016. Mustafa also authored *Hands-On Cloud Administration in Azure* and *Azure Networking Cookbook*, and the coauthored *Learn Node.js with Azure*, all published by Packt.

Tom Janetscheck is a cloud security expert from Germany. He has more than 15 years of experience in designing, building, and monitoring on premises and cloud infrastructure solutions, and a focus on security architecture in the Microsoft cloud, making him a resource on all things Azure and enterprise security.

Tom is a well-known international conference speaker with a proven track record of attendee satisfaction. Since 2017, he received the Microsoft MVP award several times for his extraordinary community contributions in the area of Microsoft Azure Security.

In his spare time, Tom is an enthusiastic motorcyclist, scuba diver, guitarist, bass player, drummer, and station officer at the local fire department.

About the reviewer

Sasha Kranjac is a cloud and security expert, architect, and instructor with more than 2 decades of experience in the field. He began programming in Assembler on Sir Clive Sinclair's ZX, met Windows NT 3.5, and the love has existed ever since. Sasha owns an IT training and consulting company that helps companies embrace the cloud and be safe in cyberspace. Aside from cloud/security architecture and consulting, he delivers Microsoft, EC-Council, and his own bespoke Azure and security courses and PowerClass workshops internationally. Sasha is a Microsoft MVP, Microsoft Certified Trainer (MCT), MCT Regional Lead, Certified EC-Council Instructor (CEI), and a frequent speaker at various international conferences, user groups, and events.

Packt is searching for authors like you

If you're interested in becoming an author for Packt, please visit authors.packtpub.com and apply today. We have worked with thousands of developers and tech professionals, just like you, to help them share their insight with the global tech community. You can make a general application, apply for a specific hot topic that we are recruiting an author for, or submit your own idea.

Table of Contents

3
Managing Cloud Identities

Section 2:
Cloud Infrastructure Security

4
Azure Network Security

5

Azure Key Vault

6

Data Security

Section 3:
Security Management

7

Azure Security Center

8

Azure Sentinel

9

Security Best Practices

Assessments

Other Books You May Enjoy

Index

Preface

Security is always integrated into a cloud platform and this causes users to let their guard down as they take cloud security for granted. Cloud computing brings new security challenges, but you can overcome these with Microsoft Azure's shared responsibility model.

Mastering Azure Security covers the latest security features provided by Microsoft to identify different threats and protect your Azure cloud using innovative techniques. The book takes you through the built-in security controls and the multi-layered security features offered by Azure to protect cloud workloads across apps and networks. You'll get to grips with using Azure Security Center for unified security management, building secure applications on Azure, protecting the cloud from DDoS attacks, safeguarding sensitive information with Azure Key Vault, and much more. Additionally, the book covers Azure Sentinel, monitoring and auditing, Azure security and governance best practices, and secure resource deployments.

By the end of this book, you'll have developed a solid understanding of cybersecurity in the cloud and be able to design secure solutions in Microsoft Azure.

Who this book is for?

This book is for Azure cloud professionals, Azure architects, and security professionals looking to implement safe and secure cloud services using Azure Security Center and other Azure security features. A fundamental understanding of security concepts and prior exposure to the Azure cloud will assist with understanding the key concepts covered in the book.

What this book covers

Chapter 1, Introduction to Azure Security, covers how the cloud is changing the concept of IT, and security is not an exception. Cybersecurity requires a different approach in the cloud and we need to understand what the differences are, new threats, and how to tackle them.

Chapter 2, Governance and Security, goes into how to create policies and rules in Microsoft Azure in order to create standards, enforcing these policies and rules, and maintaining quality levels.

Chapter 3, Managing Cloud Identities, explains why identity is one of the most important parts of security. With the cloud, identity is even more expressed than ever before. You'll learn how to keep identities secure and safe in Microsoft Azure and how to keep track of access rights and monitor any anomalies in user behavior.

Chapter 4, Azure Network Security, covers how the network is the first line of defense in any environment. Keeping resources safe and unreachable by attackers is a very important part of security. You'll learn how to achieve this in Microsoft Azure with built-in or custom tools.

Chapter 5, Azure KeyVault, explains how to manage secrets and certificates in Azure and deploy resources to Microsoft Azure with Infrastructure as Code in a secure way.

Chapter 6, Data Security, covers how to protect data in the cloud with additional encryption using Microsoft or your own encryption key.

Chapter 7, Azure Security Center, explains how to use ASC to detect threats in Microsoft Azure and how to view assessments, reports, and recommendations in order to increase Azure tenant security. It also looks at how to increase VM security by enabling just-in-time access.

Chapter 8, Azure Sentinel, covers how to use Azure Sentinel to monitor security for your Azure and on-premise resources, including detecting threats before they happen and using artificial intelligence to analyze and investigate threats. Using Azure Sentinel to automate responses to security threats and stop them immediately is also covered.

Chapter 9, Security Best Practices, introduces best practices for Azure security, including how to set up a bulletproof Azure environment, finding the hidden security features that are placed all over Azure, and other tools that may help you increase security in Microsoft Azure.

To get the most out of this book

You will require the following software, which is open source and free to use, except for Microsoft Azure, which is subscription-based and billed based on usage per minute. However, even for Microsoft Azure, a trial subscription can be used.

Software/Hardware covered in the book	OS Requirements
A Microsoft Azure subscription	Windows, macOS X, and Linux (any)
PowerShell	Windows, macOS X, and Linux (any)
Azure PowerShell	Windows, macOS X, and Linux (any)
The Azure CLI	Windows, macOS X, and Linux (any)
Visual Studio Code	Windows, macOS X, and Linux (any)

If you are using the digital version of this book, we advise you to type the code yourself or access the code via the GitHub repository (link available in the next section). Doing so will help you avoid any potential errors related to the copy/pasting of code.

Download the example code files

You can download the example code files for this book from your account at www.packt.com. If you purchased this book elsewhere, you can visit www.packtpub.com/support and register to have the files emailed directly to you.

You can download the code files by following these steps:

1. Log in or register at www.packt.com.
2. Select the **Support** tab.
3. Click on **Code Downloads**.
4. Enter the name of the book in the **Search** box and follow the onscreen instructions.

Once the file is downloaded, please make sure that you unzip or extract the folder using the latest version of:

-   WinRAR/7-Zip for Windows
-   Zipeg/iZip/UnRarX for Mac
-   7-Zip/PeaZip for Linux

The code bundle for the book is also hosted on GitHub at `https://github.com/PacktPublishing/Mastering-Azure-Security`. In case there's an update to the code, it will be updated on the existing GitHub repository.

We also have other code bundles from our rich catalog of books and videos available at `https://github.com/PacktPublishing/`. Check them out!

Download the color images

We also provide a PDF file that has color images of the screenshots/diagrams used in this book. You can download it here: `http://www.packtpub.com/sites/default/files/downloads/9781839218996_ColorImages.pdf`.

Conventions used

There are a number of text conventions used throughout this book.

`Code in text`: Indicates code words in text, database table names, folder names, filenames, file extensions, pathnames, dummy URLs, user input, and Twitter handles. Here is an example: "How to create a rule to deny traffic over port 22"

A block of code is set as follows:

```
"policyRule": {
"if": {
        "not": {
                "field": "location",
"in": "[parameters('allowedLocations')]"
}
},
"then": {
        "effect": "deny"
}
}
```

Any command-line input or output is written as follows:

```
New-AzResourceGroup -Name "Packt-Security" -Location `
"westeurope"
```

Bold: Indicates a new term, an important word, or words that you see onscreen. For example, words in menus or dialog boxes appear in the text like this. Here is an example: "Go to the **Subnet** section under **NSG** and select **Associate**."

> **Tips or important notes**
> Appear like this.

Get in touch

Feedback from our readers is always welcome.

General feedback: If you have questions about any aspect of this book, mention the book title in the subject of your message and email us at customercare@packtpub.com.

Errata: Although we have taken every care to ensure the accuracy of our content, mistakes do happen. If you have found a mistake in this book, we would be grateful if you would report this to us. Please visit www.packtpub.com/support/errata, selecting your book, clicking on the Errata Submission Form link, and entering the details.

Piracy: If you come across any illegal copies of our works in any form on the Internet, we would be grateful if you would provide us with the location address or website name. Please contact us at copyright@packt.com with a link to the material.

If you are interested in becoming an author: If there is a topic that you have expertise in and you are interested in either writing or contributing to a book, please visit authors.packtpub.com.

Reviews

Please leave a review. Once you have read and used this book, why not leave a review on the site that you purchased it from? Potential readers can then see and use your unbiased opinion to make purchase decisions, we at Packt can understand what you think about our products, and our authors can see your feedback on their book. Thank you!

For more information about Packt, please visit packt.com.

Section 1:
Identity and
Governance

In this section, you will learn how to create and enforce policies in Azure, how to manage and secure identity in Azure, and what is cybersecurity in the cloud.

This section comprises the following chapters:

1
Introduction to Azure security

When cloud computing comes up as the subject of a conversation, security is, very often, the main topic. When data leaves local datacenters, many wonder what happens to it. We are used to having complete control over everything, from physical servers, networks, and hypervisors, to applications and data. Then, all of a sudden, we are supposed to transfer much of that to someone else. It's natural to feel a little tension and distrust at the beginning, but, if we dig deep, we'll see that cloud computing can offer us more security than we could ever achieve on our own.

Microsoft Azure is a cloud computing service provided through Microsoft-managed datacenters dispersed around the world. Azure datacenters are built to top industry standards and comply with all the relevant certification authorities, such as ISO/IEC 27001:2013 and NIST SP 800-53, to name a couple. These standards guarantee that Microsoft Azure is built to provide security and reliability.

In this chapter, we'll learn about Azure security concepts and how security is structured in Microsoft Azure datacenters, using the following topics:

- Exploring the shared responsibility model
- Physical security
- Azure network

- Azure infrastructure availability

- Azure infrastructure integrity

- Azure infrastructure monitoring

- Understanding Azure security foundations

Exploring the shared responsibility model

While Microsoft Azure is very secure, responsibility for building a secure environment doesn't rest with Microsoft alone. Its shared responsibility model divides responsibility between Microsoft and its customers.

Before we can discuss which party looks after which aspect of security, we need to first discuss cloud service models. There are three basic models:

- **Infrastructure as a Service (IaaS)**

- **Platform as a Service (PaaS)**

- **Software as a Service (SaaS)**

These models differ in terms of what is controlled by Microsoft and the customer. A general break up can be seen in the following diagram:

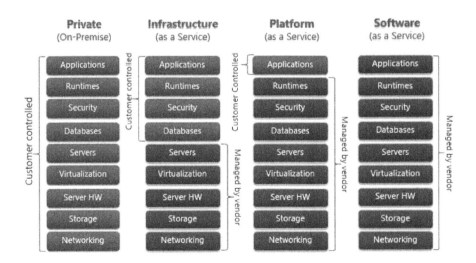

Figure 1.1 – Basic cloud service models

Let's look at these services in a little more detail:

On-premises

In an on-premises environment, we, as users, take care of everything: the network, physical servers, storage, and so on. We need to set up virtualization stacks (if used), configure and maintain servers, install and maintain software, manage databases, and so on. Most importantly, all aspects of security are our responsibility: physical security, network security, host and OS security, and application security for all application software running on our servers.

Infrastructure as a Service

With IaaS, Microsoft takes over some of the responsibilities. We only take care of data, runtime, applications, and some aspects of security, which we'll discuss a little later on. An example of an IaaS product in Microsoft Azure is Azure **Virtual Machines** (**VM**).

Platform as a Service

PaaS gives Microsoft even more responsibility. We only take care of our applications. However, this still means looking after a part of the security. Some examples of PaaS in Microsoft Azure are Azure SQL Database and web apps.

Software as a Service

SaaS gives a large amount of control away, and we manage very little, including some aspects of security. In Microsoft's ecosystem, a popular example of SaaS is Office365; however, we will not discuss this in this book.

Now that we have a basic understanding of shared responsibility, let's understand how responsibility for security is allocated.

Division of security in the shared responsibility model

The shared responsibility model divides security into three zones:

- Always controlled by the customer
- Always controlled by Microsoft
- Varies by service type

Irrespective of the cloud service model, customers will always retain the following security responsibilities:

- Data governance and right management
- Endpoints
- Account and access management

Similarly, Microsoft always handles the following, in terms of security, for any of its cloud service models:

- Physical datacenter
- Physical network
- Physical hosts

Finally, there are a few security responsibilities that are allocated based on the cloud service model:

- Identity and directory infrastructure
- Applications
- Network
- Operating system

Responsibility distribution, based on different cloud service models, is shown in the following diagram:

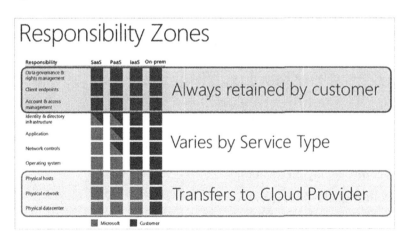

Figure 1.2 – Responsibility distribution between the customer and service provider for different cloud service models (image courtesy of Microsoft, License: MIT)

Now that we know how security is divided, let's move on to one specific aspect of it: the physical security that Microsoft manages. This section is important as we won't discuss it in much detail in the chapters to come.

Physical security

It all starts with physical security. No matter what we do to protect our data from attacks coming from outside of our network, it would all be in vain if someone was to walk into datacenters or server rooms and take away disks from our servers. Microsoft takes physical security very seriously in order to reduce risk from unauthorized access to data and datacenter resources.

Azure datacenters can be accessed only through strictly defined access points. A facility's perimeter is safeguarded by tall fences made of steel and concrete. In order to enter Azure datacenters, a person needs to go through at least two checkpoints: first to enter the facility perimeter, and second to enter the building. Both checkpoints are staffed by professional and trained security personnel. In addition to the access points, security personnel patrol the facility's perimeter. The facility and its buildings are covered by video surveillance, which is monitored by the security personnel.

After entering the building, two-factor authentication with biometrics is required to gain access to the inside of the datacenter. If their identity is validated, a person can access only approved parts of the datacenter. Approval, besides defining areas that can be accessed, also defines periods that can be spent inside these areas. It also strictly defines whether a person can access these areas alone or needs to be accompanied by someone.

Before accessing each area inside the datacenter, a mandatory metal detector check is performed. In order to prevent unauthorized data leaving or entering the datacenter, only approved devices are allowed. Additionally, all server racks are monitored from the front and back using video surveillance. When leaving a datacenter area, an additional metal detector screening is required. This helps Microsoft make sure that nothing that can compromise its data's security is brought in or removed from the datacenter without authorization.

A review of physical security is conducted periodically for all facilities. This aims to satisfy all security requirements at all times.

After equipment reaches the end of its life, it is disposed of in a secure way, with rigorous data and hardware disposal policies. During the disposal process, Microsoft personnel ensure that data is not available to untrusted parties. All data devices are either wiped (if possible) or physically destroyed in order to render the recovery of any information impossible.

All Microsoft Azure datacenters are designed, built, and operated in a way that satisfies top industry standards, such as ISO 27001, HIPAA, FedRAMP, SOC 1, and SOC 2, to name a few. In many cases, specific region or country standards are followed as well, such as Australia IRAP, UK GCloud, and Singapore MTCS.

As an added precaution, all data inside any Microsoft Azure datacenter is encrypted at rest. Even if someone managed to get their hands on disks with customers' data, which is virtually impossible with all the security measures, it would take an enormous effort (both from a financial and time perspective) to decrypt any of the data.

But in the cloud era, network security is equally, if not more, important as physical security. Most services are accessed over the internet, and even isolated services depend on the network layer. So next, we need to take a look at Azure network architecture.

Azure network

Networking in Azure can be separated into two parts: managed by Microsoft and managed by us. In this section, we will discuss the part of networking managed by Microsoft. It's important to understand the architecture, reliability, and security setup of this part to provide more context once we move to parts of network security that we need to manage.

As with Azure datacenters generally, the Azure network follows industry standards with three distinct models/layers:

- Core
- Distribution
- Access

All three models use distinct hardware in order to completely separate all the layers. The core layer uses datacenter routers, the distribution layer uses access routers and L2 aggregation (this layer separates L3 routing from L2 switching), and the access layer uses L2 switches.

Azure network architecture includes two levels of L2 switches:

- **First level**: Aggregates traffic
- **Second level**: Loops to incorporate redundancy

This approach allows for more flexibility and better port scaling. Another benefit of this approach is that L2 and L3 are totally separated, which allows for the use of distinct hardware for each layer in the network. Distinct hardware minimizes the chances of a fault in one layer affecting another one. The use of trunks allows for resource sharing for better connectivity.

The network inside an Azure datacenter is distributed into clusters for better control, scaling, and fault tolerance. Each network in every Azure cluster consists of the following devices:

- Routers
- Switches
- Digi CMs
- Power distribution units

Routers can be separated into three groups: datacenter, access, and border leaf routers. Switches are aggregation or top-of-rack switches.

It's important to mention that there are two different network architectures in Azure datacenters – **Default LAN Architecture (DLA)** and **Quantum 10 Architecture (Q10)**.

DLA is used by some existing customers and shared services, mainly in some of the first Azure regions. Q10 is used in newer Azure datacenters and virtual customers. DLA uses a classic tree design with active/passive access routers. Q10 uses a close/mesh design. The main difference between these architectures is how **Access Control Lists (ACLs)** are applied. In DLA, ACLs are applied directly to access routers. Q10 doesn't apply ACLs on the routing level but one level below, using software-defined networking with **Software Load Balancing (SLBs)** and software-defined VLANs.

The main benefit of Q10 is its greater capability and ability to scale existing infrastructure. Another benefit of Q10 is that software-defined networking can handle some security features, such as **Network Address Translation (NAT)**.

Both architectures, DLA and Q10, are shown in the following diagram:

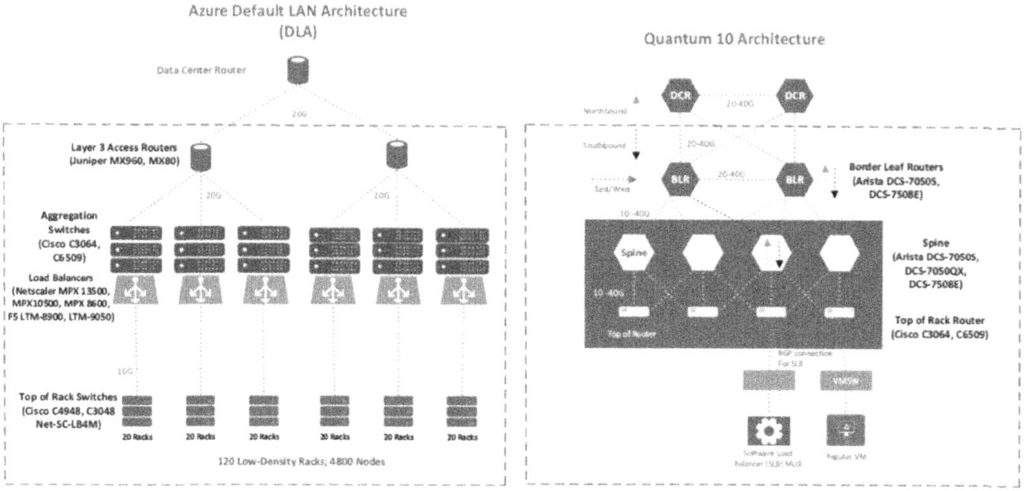

Figure 1.3 – DLA and Quantum 10 architecture (image courtesy of Microsoft, License: MIT)

Azure networking is built upon highly redundant infrastructure in each Azure datacenter. Implemented redundancy is **need plus one** (**N+1**) or better, with full failover features within and between Azure datacenters. Full failover tolerance ensures constant network and service availability. From the outside, Azure datacenters are connected by dedicated, high-bandwidth network circuits redundantly that connect properties with over 1,200 **Internet Service Providers** (**ISPs**) on a global level. Edge capacity across the network is over 2,000 GBps, which presents an enormous network potential.

Distributed Denial of Service (**DDoS**) is becoming a huge issue in terms of service availability. As the number of cloud services increases, DDoS attacks become more targeted and sophisticated. With the help of geographical distribution and quick detection, Microsoft can help you mitigate these DDoS attacks and minimize the impact. Let's take a look at this in more detail.

Azure infrastructure availability

Azure is designed, built, and operated in order to deliver highly available and reliable infrastructure. Improvements are constantly implemented to increase availability and reliability, along with efficiency and scalability. Delivery of a more secure and trusted cloud is always a priority.

Uninterruptible power supplies and vast banks of batteries ensure that the flow of electricity stays uninterrupted in case of short-term power disruptions. In the case of long-term power disruptions, emergency generators can provide backup power for days. Emergency power generators are used in cases of long power outages or planned maintenance. In cases of natural disasters, when the external power supply is unavailable for long periods of time, each Azure datacenter has fuel reserves on-site.

Robust and high-speed fiber-optic networks connect datacenters to major hubs. It's important that, along with connection through major hubs, datacenters are connected directly between themselves as well. Everything is distributed into nodes, which host workloads closer to users to reduce latency, provide geo-redundancy, and increase resiliency.

Data in Azure can be placed in two separate locations: primary and secondary locations. A customer can choose where primary and secondary locations will be. The secondary location is a backup site. In each location, primary and secondary, Azure keeps three healthy copies of your data at all times. This means that six copies of data are available at any time. If any data copy becomes unavailable at any time, it's immediately declared invalid, a new copy is created, and the old one is destroyed.

Microsoft ensures high availability and reliability through constant monitoring, incident response, and service support. Each Azure datacenter operates 24/7/365 to ensure that everything is running and all services are available at all times. Of course, "available at all times" is a goal that, ultimately, is impossible to reach. There are many circumstances that can impact uptime, and sometimes it's impossible to control all of them. Realistically, the aim is to achieve the best possible **Service Level Agreement** (**SLA**) and ensure that potential downtime is as small as possible. The SLA can vary on a number of factors and is different per service and configuration. If we take into account all the factors we can control, the best SLA we can achieve would be 99.99%, also known as "four nines."

Closely connected to infrastructure availability is infrastructure integrity. Integrity affects the availability terms of deployment, where all steps must be verified from different perspectives. New deployments must not cause any downtime or affect existing services in any way.

Azure infrastructure integrity

All software components installed in the Azure environment are custom built. This, of course, refers to software installed and managed by Microsoft as part of Azure Service Fabric. Custom software is built using Microsoft's **Security Development Lifecycle** (**SDL**) process, including operating system images and SQL databases. All software deployment is conducted as part of the strictly defined change management and release management process. All nodes and fabric controllers use customized versions of Windows Server 2012. Installation of any unauthorized software is not allowed.

VMs running in Azure are grouped into clusters. Each cluster contains around 1,000 VMs. All VMs are managed by the **Fabric Controller** (**FC**). The FC is scaled out and redundant. Each FC is responsible for the life cycle management of applications running in its own cluster. This includes provisioning and monitoring of hardware in that cluster. If any server fails, the FC automatically rebuilds a new instance of that server.

Each Azure software component undergoes a build process (as part of the release management process) that includes virus scans using endpoint protection anti-virus tools. As each software component undergoes this process, nothing goes to production without a clean-virus scan. During the release management process, all components go through a build process. During this process, an anti-virus scan is performed. Each virus scan creates a log in the build directory and, if any issues are detected, the process for this component is frozen. Any software components for which the issue is detected undergo inspection by Microsoft security teams in order to detect the exact issue.

Azure is a closed and locked-down environment. All nodes and guest VMs have their default Windows administrator account disabled. No user accounts are created directly on any of the nodes or guest VMs as well. Administrators from Azure support can connect to them only with proper authorization to perform maintenance tasks and emergency repairs.

With all precautions taken to provide maximum availability and security, incidents may occur from time to time. In order to detect these issues and mitigate them as soon as possible, Microsoft implemented monitoring and incident management.

Azure infrastructure monitoring

All hardware, software, and network devices in Azure datacenters are constantly reviewed and updated. Reviews and updates are performed mandatorily at least once a year, but additional reviews and updates are performed as needed. Any changes (to hardware, software, or the network) must go through the release management process and need to be developed, tested, and approved in development and test environments prior to release to production. In this process, all changes must be reviewed and approved by the Azure security and compliance team.

All Azure datacenters use integrated deployment systems for the distribution and installation of security updates for all software provided by Microsoft. If third-party software is used, the customer or software manufacturer is responsible for security updates, depending on how the software is provided and used. For example, if third-party software is installed using Azure Marketplace, the manufacturer is responsible for providing updates. If software is manually installed, then it depends on the specific software. For Microsoft software, a special team within Microsoft, named **Microsoft Security Response Center**, is responsible for monitoring and identifying any security incident 24/7/365. Furthermore, any incident must be resolved in the shortest possible time frame.

Vulnerability scanning is performed across the Azure infrastructure (servers, databases, and network) at least once every quarter. If there is a specific issue or incident, vulnerability scanning is performed more often. Microsoft performs penetration tests, but also hires independent consultants to perform penetration tests. This ensures that nothing goes undetected. Any security issues are addressed immediately in order to increase security and stop any exploit when the issue is detected.

In case of any security issue, Microsoft has incident management in place. In the case where Microsoft is aware of a security issue, it takes the following actions:

1. The customer is notified of the incident.
2. An immediate investigation is started in order to provide detailed information regarding the security incident.
3. Steps are taken to mitigate the effects and minimize the damage of the security incident.

Incident management is clearly defined in order to manage, escalate, and resolve all security incidents promptly.

Understanding Azure security foundations

Overall, we can see that with Microsoft Azure, the cloud can be very secure. But it's very important to understand the shared responsibility model as well. Just putting applications and data into the cloud doesn't make it secure. Microsoft provides certain parts of security and ensures that physical and network security is in place. Customers must assume part of the responsibility and ensure that the right measures are taken on their side as well.

For example, let's say we place our database and application in Microsoft Azure, but our application is vulnerable to SQL injection (still a very common method of data breach). Can we blame Microsoft if our data is breached?

Let's be more extreme and say we publicly exposed the endpoint and forgot to put in place any kind of authentication. Is this Microsoft's responsibility?

If we look at the level of physical and network security that Microsoft provides in Azure datacenters, not many organizations can say that they have the same level in their local datacenters. More often than not, physical security is totally neglected. Server rooms are not secure, access is not controlled, and many times there is not even a dedicated server room, but just server racks in some corner or corridor. Even when a server room is under lock, no change of management is in place, and no one controls or reviews who is entering the server room and why. On the other hand, Microsoft implements top-level security in their datacenters. Everything is under constant surveillance, and every access needs to be approved and reviewed. Even if something is missed, everything is still encrypted and additionally secured. In my experience, this is again something that most organizations don't bother with.

Similar things can be said about network security. In most organizations, almost all network security is gone after the firewall. Networks are usually unsegmented, no traffic control is in place inside the network, and so on. Routing and traffic forwarding are basic or non-existent. Microsoft Azure again addresses these problems very well and helps us have secure networks for our resources.

But even with all the components of security that Microsoft takes care of, this is only the beginning. Using Microsoft Azure, we can achieve better physical and network security than we could in local datacenters, and we can concentrate on other things.

The shared responsibility model has different responsibilities for different cloud service models, and it's sometimes unclear what needs to be done. Luckily, even if it's not Microsoft's responsibility to address these parts of security, there are many security services available in Azure. Many of Azure's services have the single purpose of addressing security and helping us protect our data and resources in Azure datacenters. Again, it does not stop there. Most of Azure's services have some sort of security features built in, even when these services are not security-related. Microsoft takes security very seriously and enables us to secure our resources with many different tools.

The tools available vary from tools that help us to increase security by simply enabling a number of options, to tools that have lots of configuration options that help us design security, to tools that monitor our Azure resources and give us security recommendations that we need to implement. Some Azure tools use machine learning to help us detect security incidents in real time, or even before they happen.

This book will cover all aspects of Microsoft Azure security, from governance and identity, to network and data protection, to advanced tools. The final goal is to understand cloud security, to learn how to combine different tools to maximize security, and finally, to master Azure security!

Summary

The most important lesson in this chapter is to understand the shared responsibility model in Azure. Microsoft takes care of some parts of security, especially in terms of physical security, but we need to take care of the rest.

With Azure networking, integrity, availability, and monitoring, we don't have influence and can't change anything (at least in the sections we discussed here). However, they are important to understand as we can apply a lot of things in the parts of security that we can manage. They will also provide more context and help us to better understand the complete security setup in Azure.

In the next chapter, we will move on to identity, which is one of the most important pillars of security. In Azure, identity is even more important, as most services are managed and accessible over the internet. Therefore, we need to take additional steps in order to make identity and access secure and bulletproof.

Questions

1. Whose responsibility is security in the cloud?

    A. User's

    B. Cloud provider's

    C. Responsibility is shared

2. According to the shared responsibility model, who is responsible for the security of physical hosts?

    A. User

    B. Cloud provider

    C. Both

3. According to the shared responsibility model, who is responsible for the physical network?

    A. User

    B. Cloud provider

    C. Depends on the service model

4. According to the shared responsibility model, who is responsible for network controls?

    A. User

    B. Cloud provider

    C. Depends on the service model

5. According to the shared responsibility model, who is responsible for data governance?

    A. User

    B. Cloud provider

    C. Depends on the service model

6. Which architecture is used for Azure networking?

    A. DLA

    B. Quantum 10 (Q10)

    C. Both, but DLA is replacing Q10

    D. Both, but Q10 is replacing DLA

7. In case of a security incident, what is the first step?

    A. Immediate investigation

    B. Mitigation

    C. Customer is notified

2
Governance and Security

Before digging deep into technical features that help to secure and protect your cloud environments on Azure, we first need to stop, reflect, plan, and act accordingly. Governance is essential and you need guardrails in the cloud. When talking about cloud computing, customers often exhibit a kind of *let's get started* mentality. That's great, but in the cloud, there also need to be rules. In addition to that, you surely don't want to end up with a cloud construct that does not entirely fit your company's needs, do you?

With this chapter, we want to help you design the foundation for a secure cloud strategy and act according to your plan by leading you through the following topics:

- Understanding governance in Azure
- Using common sense to avoid mistakes
- Using management locks
- Using management groups for governance
- Understanding Azure Policy
- Defining Azure blueprints
- Azure Resource Graph

Understanding governance in Azure

If we take a deeper look at what governance actually means, we find a good definition in the online business dictionary. The first part of this definition is as follows:

Establishment of policies, and continuous monitoring of their proper implementation, by the members of the governing body of an organization.

To read the entire definition, go to the following link: `http://www.businessdictionary.com/definition/governance.html`

The most important words in this definition are *policies*, *monitoring*, and *implementation*. If you switch *implementation* for *deployment*, you get three aspects that are essential for security. So, you could say that governance is essential for security!

What's true in real life is true within the context of IT, too. I'm talking about rules. Rules only really work if they are enforced by *policies*. You can tell your administrators what they are not allowed to do. But if they can do what they are not allowed to, they are still able to accidentally break your rules. So, you need to define policies that help you to enforce or to monitor your corporate rules.

Monitoring is the second important part in terms of security. If you don't see what happens, you have no chance to react or make the right decisions. This is why monitoring is so important and there is no way around it. In later chapters, we will cover some monitoring best practices for Azure that will help you to get the right amount of information for your environments.

Finally, there is *implementation*. You can use the Azure portal to manually deploy Azure resources. However, with that approach, you will definitely need a tight set of policies that enforce your rules so that manual deployments will not break them. If you want to make sure that all environments will strictly adhere to your rules, automatic deployments are your way to go. With a robust governance plan with policies and **role-based access controls** (**RBAC**), and by using deployments from a DevOps pipeline, such as Azure DevOps, you can make sure that your deployments and the target environment will be consistent. If you then make sure that changes to your environment can only be done from your DevOps pipeline tool, but never manually from the Azure portal, you are on your way to protecting your environments from inadvertent changes. You can use PowerShell for *imperative* deployments or **Azure Resource Manager** (**ARM**) templates, and Terraform for *declarative* deployments. Whatever best fits your needs, use it!

> **Important Note: Different deployment models**
>
> If you're using imperative scripting languages such as PowerShell to deploy resources, you need to explicitly describe what should be done in order to get the infrastructure you want. You need to define the steps in the correct order. With declarative languages such as ARM templates or Terraform, you only describe what resources have to be deployed to your target environment, so it's not about the *how* but about the *what*. We will cover examples for all of these languages later in this book.

With Azure, and with cloud computing in general, we need new approaches for security and management on the one hand, but, on the other hand, there are traditional, decades-old industry principles that still are valid. There is the principle of least privilege, or POLP. This principle states that programs or users should have the least number of privileges necessary to complete their tasks.

Segregation of duties, or SoD, is another principle that is still valid even in the cloud era. SoD is the concept of having more than one person required to complete a task. For example, you might have a team that is responsible for creating and managing accounts in Azure Active Directory, but another team that is responsible for Office 365 Management, and thus for creating user mailboxes. A third team might take care of Azure resources. In this resource team, there are administrators who manage databases, other people that take care of networks, and then there are your VM specialists managing only compute resources. SoD is also part of multi-step approvals. For example, when one of your administrators requests a role they are eligible for, someone else has to approve that request:

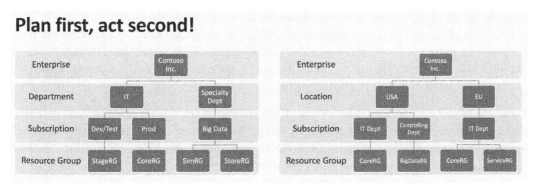

Figure. 2.1 – Plan first, act second – defining a possible Azure hierarchy

When starting your cloud journey with Microsoft Azure, the first thing to do is plan your Azure hierarchy, which describes how Azure subscriptions, tenants, and directories depend on each other in an enterprise environment. The idea is to have only one contract for one enterprise, but to have several Azure subscriptions. Every Azure subscription is tied to exactly one Azure Active Directory tenant (of which you ideally also only have one!). What you may want to do is divide your company into locations, such as Europe and North America. Alternatively, you may want to divide your company based on departments, such as IT and finance departments. You may want to do both – or you could even choose another hierarchy. Whatever fits your needs, go for it and do it before actually starting. There are three high-level hierarchy patterns: *functional*, in which subscriptions are created based on enterprise departments, such as IT and accounting; *business unit,* which can be used to differentiate between business units, such as aerospace and automotive; and *geographic,* in which subscriptions are created based on a company's geolocations. The hierarchy you go for should match your enterprise's management and geographics so that it supports you in granting access and billing according to your company's needs.

Now that you know what governance is and why it is important, let's move on and see what tools we have to make our lives easier in terms of governance and security.

Using common sense to avoid mistakes

I have often been asked how I make sure that an Azure administrator does not accidentally delete productive resources in the cloud. The answer, besides the use of technical features to be discussed in the next section, is that *common sense* helps a lot! You don't accidentally walk into your on-premises data center and pull one of your servers out of its rack and throw it out of a window, do you? You usually do not run a *nuke all* script against your Hyper-V farm just to wonder where all your VMs have gone later that day, do you? And you surely do not accidentally erase your productive SAN! On Azure, you cannot accidentally delete a resource group.

Well, you can, if you accidentally confirm the "Are you sure?" dialog and then accidentally enter the resource group's name into the prompt. Resources are even more easily removed – either by accident or by intention. So, we need something that helps us to reduce the risk of accidents. Common sense and a good sense of caution are the first steps toward a successful governance approach in the cloud.

However, even when being careful, you can still accidentally delete stuff that you shouldn't. For example, you could accidentally delete single resources, such as a storage account, a key vault, or whatever else. I remember one summer afternoon about 10 years ago when I was running a Linux firewall distribution on a small-sized hardware mainboard, comparable with today's Raspberry Pi's. I used this tiny piece of hardware as my home firewall solution and it was doing a great job. It had three local area network connections for three different networks, there was even a Wi-Fi-module onboard, and the OS was installed on a CF card. Only the RAM was limited and since the CF card was exclusively reserved for the OS installation, all logs were written on a RAM disk. This is why I had to regularly delete log files from the /var/log/* directories. I did not want to enable log rotation, but rather I wanted to export logs to another Linux server that was running in my environment. Well, long story short, what I can tell you is that running the following command while having elevated rights works pretty well – even if you have not changed your working directory to the intended one:

```
rm -rf *
```

So, I had one more Saturday afternoon reinstalling and reconfiguring the firewall. Next time, think before you act! Lesson learned.

In the next section, we will explore a technical feature to prevent administrators from accidentally deleting Azure resources.

Using management locks

Of course, there is a technical feature that prevents you from accidentally deleting anything on Azure – a feature called *management locks*. There are two different types of lock in Azure:

- *Delete* locks ensure that no one can delete resources from your Azure subscription, by accident or on purpose. Authorized users can still read and modify a resource, but they can no longer delete it.

- *ReadOnly* locks make sure that only authorized users are able to read a resource, but also that they cannot modify it nor delete it.

In every subscription I create, I usually use a **core resource group** to which I deploy resources that are used across several other resource groups. For example, if I have a virtual network that is used by several services across an entire subscription, or a key vault in which I store administrative credentials as secrets, then these types of resources are created in one of my core resource groups. As you can imagine, the resources there are very important, and so I always use a Delete lock on the scope of this core resource group.

When talking about scopes in this chapter, we are talking about management hierarchies. Locks, policies, and access rights always apply to a particular scope and they are always applied from the top down:

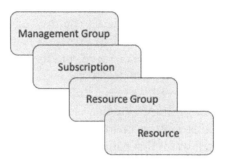

Figure. 2.2 – Azure scope from the top down: management group, subscription, resource group, and single resource

If you create a lock at the subscription level, it will apply to all resource groups and to all resources within that particular subscription. If you create it at the resource group level, it will only apply to resources within that particular resource group:

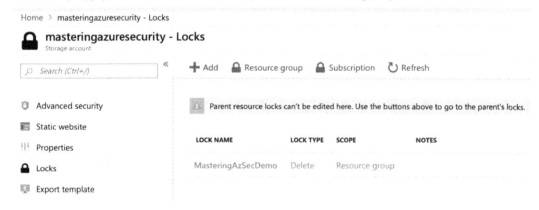

Figure. 2.3 – Azure management locks on a resource group

To demonstrate, I have created a storage account, **masteringazuresecurity**, in one of my core resources groups. If you selected **Locks** in the left management pane, you would see that someone has created a **Delete** lock with the name **MasteringAzSecDemo** at the resource group level. When you now try to delete the storage account, the following message will appear:

Figure. 2.4 – Warning message when trying to delete a locked resource

> **Important Note:**
>
> You can only create or delete management locks when you have access to the `Microsoft.Authorization/*` or `Microsoft.Authorization/locks/*` management actions. There are several built-in roles in Azure, of which only *Owner* and *User Access Administrator* are granted those particular management actions.

Now you know how management locks are used in Azure and about the scopes that can be used to create them. In the next section, we will explore using management groups, one of the most important levels of scope, and how you can leverage them to define your cloud governance.

Using management groups for governance

As mentioned previously, it is essential to have a plan and stick to it in terms of governance, guardrails, rules, and policies. Organizations that use many subscriptions need an efficient way to manage access, policies, and compliance rules for all their subscriptions. With Azure management groups, we are given a level of scope above the subscription level:

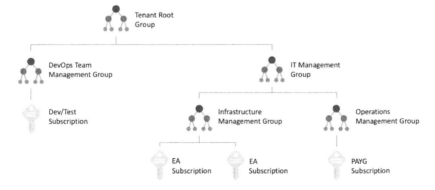

Figure. 2.5 – Example of a management group hierarchy

With management groups, we can configure different management scopes that allow us to granularly manage all governance settings with little effort. The preceding diagram shows a possible management group hierarchy. As you can see, a management group can contain both subscriptions and other management groups. The example shows a hierarchy in which several types of subscriptions have been created and attached to different management groups. You can have **pay-as-you-go** (**PAYG**) subscriptions, **enterprise agreement** (**EA**) subscriptions, and **dev/test** subscriptions in a single tenant and attach them to any of your management groups.

Maybe you want to make sure that all the resources you create in Azure for production are only stored in both of the European Azure regions, West Europe and North Europe. In this scenario, you can create a management group that contains all your production subscriptions and then apply a policy to the management group that limits resource creation to only those regions. Another scenario for management groups might be to provide user access to several Azure subscriptions at once instead of managing access for every single subscription individually.

Each Azure AD directory is given a top-level management group called a root management group. All subscriptions and management groups that are created for this Azure tenant belong to this root group. The root management group enables customers to create global policies and role assignments that are valid for all Azure subscriptions within an Azure tenant's scope.

The root group's default display name is **Tenant Root Group**. Here are some important facts that you should know regarding a tenant root group:

- Only user accounts that have been assigned *Owner* or *Contributor* roles on the tenant root group are able to change their display name.

- The root group cannot be deleted or moved to another management group.

- In an Azure hierarchy, all subscriptions and management groups fold up to the one tenant root group in the respective directory. There is only one tenant root group, and all other management groups, subscriptions, and resources are child objects within this tenant root group. That said, all resources within all subscriptions fold up to the tenant root group for global management. New subscriptions are automatically attached to the tenant root group when created.

- No one is given default access to the tenant root group. Only Azure AD global administrators have the right to elevate themselves to gain access and to make changes if necessary.

You might want to give your security administrators read access to all resources that are created within the scope of your Azure AD tenant as they need to see all your subscriptions and management groups. Alternatively, you want to give application access to all your Azure subscriptions; for example, the ability to automatically deploy resources or to gather information about billing. Therefore, you might want to change some settings on your tenant root group so that you only have to manage access rights once. As no one is able to access a tenant root group by default, you first need to elevate access for an Azure AD Global administrator.

When elevating access for an Azure AD Global administrator, the account is assigned the User Access Management role in Azure at the root scope (/). This role at the root scope allows the account to view all resources and assign access to any subscription or management group in the whole directory!

To elevate access, carry out the following steps:

1. Sign in to the Azure portal or Azure Active Directory Admin Center as a Global administrator.

2. Click **Azure Active Directory** and then **Properties** in the navigation list:

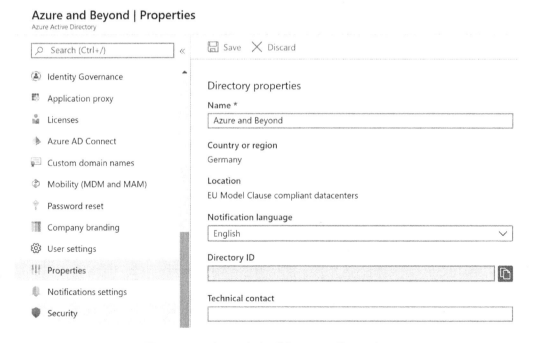

Figure. 2.6 – Azure Active Directory – Properties

3.   Under **Access management for Azure resources**, set the toggle switch to **Yes**:

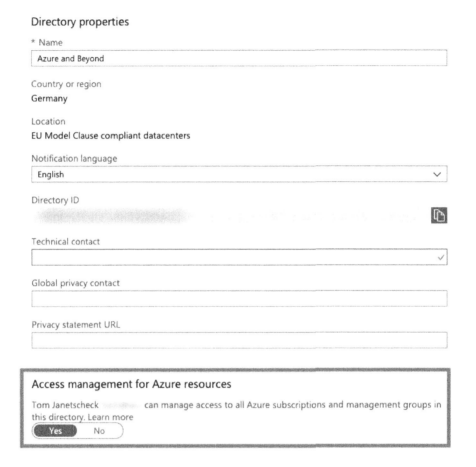

Figure. 2.7 – Enable access management for all Azure resources

> **Tip**
> Access rights should always be as restrictive as possible, and they should only
> be granted when needed. That said, be sure to remove elevated access once you
> have made your changes to the tenant root group.

To remove elevated access, either set the toggle switch back to **No** or use PowerShell to
remove the User Access Administrator role assignment from the root scope:

```
Remove-AzRoleAssignment -SignInName <username@example.com> `
    -RoleDefinitionName "User Access Administrator" -Scope "/"
```

> **Important Note:**
>
> In order to be able to execute this PowerShell command, you need to install the latest version of the Az PowerShell module. As you cannot have both the old AzureRM and new Az PowerShell modules installed in parallel, you first need to uninstall the AzureRM module. For more information, please refer to `https://docs.microsoft.com/en-us/powershell/azure`.

You just learned how management groups are used for governance. In the next section, we will look at Azure Policy, the service that enforces your rules.

Understanding Azure Policy

Rules are important, but to be sure that they are not broken, you either need to monitor their application or you need to enforce them. With Azure Policy, you get a service that you can use to achieve both. Azure Policy allows you to create, assign, and manage policies. Policies that you define enforce different rules for resources that you create in a policy's scope.

The Azure Policy service evaluates resources for non-compliance with assigned policies and then applies a defined action. For example, you may want to only allow your Azure administrators to create Azure resources in the North Europe and West Europe Azure regions, or you may only want to have a certain VM SKU size in one of your Azure subscriptions. In these cases, you can create a policy. Once this policy is created and activated, new and existing resources are evaluated for policy compliance. New resources are prevented from being created if they are non-compliant and existing resources can be brought into compliance if needed.

There are four different effect types that you can define for your policies:

- **Disabled** is useful when testing the effect of a new policy definition or when you want to disable only one assignment instead of all assignments of a particular policy definition.

- **Append** is used to add additional fields to a requested resource during resource creation or a resource update. With an append policy, you can, for example, add tags to a resource such as **resourceOwner** or **costCenter**.

- **Deny** is used to deny a resource request that does not match your compliance standard. The resource request will fail after evaluation. With a deny policy, you can, for example, prevent your administrators from creating resources in Azure regions that you do not allow, or prevent them from deploying VM SKU sizes you have not approved.

- **Audit** is used to create a warning event in the activity log when evaluating a non-compliant resource. The resource request will not be stopped, but you will be able to be informed about non-compliance.

When using Azure Policy, you might need to create a custom policy definition or use one of the built-in policy definitions that already come with Azure, such as any of these:

- **Allowed Locations:** This policy definition restricts the available locations for new resources. It is used to enforce your geo-compliance requirements.
- **Audit VMs that do not use managed disks:** This policy audits VMs that do not use managed disks. A warning event for every VM will be generated in the activity log.
- **Allowed Virtual Machine SKUs:** This definition specifies a set of VM SKUs that you can deploy.

Policy definitions describe resource compliance and what effect to use when a resource is, or becomes, non-compliant. The schema for policy definitions is documented at `https://schema.management.azure.com/schemas/2018-05-01/policyDefinition.json`. Policy definitions are created in JSON.

A policy definition contains the following elements:

- Mode
- Parameters
- Display name (as it is found in the Azure portal or in the CLI)
- Description (what this policy is actually doing, when to use it, and so on)
- Policy rule (the rule definition)
- Logical evaluation: What is the condition for resource compliance?
- Effect: What happens if a resource is non-compliant?

Mode

The policy mode determines which resource types are evaluated by the policy. There are two modes supported:

- **all**: All resource groups and resource types are evaluated.
- **indexed**: Only resource types that support tags and locations are evaluated.

If you create a policy through the Azure portal, the mode is always set to Apply. If you use PowerShell or the Azure CLI, you can specify the mode parameter manually.

> **Important Note:**
> If your custom policy definition does not include a mode value, it defaults to *all*
> in PowerShell and to *null* in the Azure CLI. The *null* value is the same as using
> *indexed* for backward-compatibility reasons.

Parameters

Parameters in a policy definition help to reduce the number of policy definitions. You
can think of them as fields in a form, such as name, surname, and street address. The
parameters always stay the same; only their values change depending on who fills the form
out. By including parameters in your policy definition, you can reuse the policy and just
change the values accordingly.

Parameter properties

A parameter has the following properties:

- `name`: The name of your parameter.
- `type`: The parameter type can be a `string`, `array`, `object`, `boolean`,
  `integer`, `float`, or `datetime`.
- `metadata`: The parameter's sub-properties used by the Azure portal to display
  user-friendly information about the parameter.
- `description`: An explanation of what the parameter is used for.
- `display name`: A friendly name for the parameter shown in the Azure portal.
- `strongType`: (Optional) This property is used when assigning the policy through
  the Azure portal. A current list of supported `strongType` options is published at
  `https://docs.microsoft.com/en-us/azure/governance/policy/`
  `concepts/definition-structure#strongtype`.
- `assignPermissions`: (Optional) If this value is set to `true`, the Azure portal
  will create role assignments during policy assignment. This option can be useful if
  you want to assign permissions outside the policy's assignment scope.
- `defaultValue`: (Optional) If no value is specified during policy assignment,
  this value is used. `defaultValue` is mandatory if you update an existing policy
  definition that is already assigned.
- `allowedValues`: (Optional) This property provides an array of values that the
  parameter will accept during policy assignment.

You may want to restrict Azure resource creation to only a few Azure regions. In a policy that is used to only allow resource creation in European Azure regions, you could define a parameter called `allowedLocations`. With each policy assignment, this parameter would be used and evaluated. With the `strongType` value defined, you would get an additional field in the Azure portal when assigning the policy:

```
"parameters": {
    "allowedLocations": {
        "type": "array",
        "metadata": {
            "description": "The list of allowed locations for
resources.",
            "displayName": "Allowed locations",
            "strongType": "location"
        },
        "defaultValue": [ "westeurope" ],
        "allowedValues": [
            "northeurope",
            "westeurope"
        ]
    }
}
```

The preceding code shows the parameter definition section in an Azure policy definition. The `allowedLocations` parameter, in this case, is an array that contains two allowed values, `northeurope` and `westeurope`. The default value is set to `westeurope`, which means that this is the location that is taken by default if you do not set the parameter to another value. Then, in the policy rule, the parameter is referenced as follows:

```
"policyRule": {
"if": {
            "not": {
                    "field": "location",
"in": "[parameters('allowedLocations')]"
    }
},
"then": {
            "effect": "deny"
    }
}
```

The whole policy definition for this purpose might look like this:

```json
{
    "properties": {
        "mode": "all",
        "parameters": {
            "allowedLocations": {
                "type": "array",
                "metadata": {
                    "description": "The list of locations that
can be specified when deploying resources",
                    "strongType": "location",
                    "displayName": "Allowed locations"
                },
                "defaultValue": [ "westeurope " ]
                "allowedValues": [
            "northeurope",
                    "westeurope"
                ]


            }
        },
        "displayName": "Allowed locations",
        "description": "With this policy you can restrict
resource creation to Azure regions your organization allows.",
        "policyRule": {
            "if": {
                "not": {
                    "field": "location",
                    "in": "[parameters('allowedLocations')]"
                }
            },
            "then": {
                "effect": "deny"
            }
        }
    }
}
```

Policy assignments

When you create a policy definition, you need to assign it to a specific scope for the policy to take effect. This is what Microsoft calls a policy assignment. The scope for a policy assignment can be anything from a management group over a subscription down to a resource group. Policy assignments are passed on from parent to child resources. So, policies that are assigned to a management group or a subscription are also applied to all downstream resources within that scope. But you can also exclude a subscope from the policy assignment. For example, say you want to prevent your administrators from creating resources outside Europe. However, you have one resource group in which you need to create IoT resources outside Europe. In this case, you could create a policy definition that only allows resource creation in one of the European Azure regions. This policy is assigned to the management group so it will be applied to all subscriptions, resource groups, and resources within that scope. Then, you exclude the one resource group with the exception from the policy assignment so the policy will not be applied to that group.

Initiative definitions

Policies are used to enforce exactly one rule. Initiatives are collections of several rules that belong together. For example, there is a pre-configured initiative definition that comes with Azure Security Center. In this initiative definition, you will find all the audit policies that will reflect in the recommendations section of Azure Security Center, which is covered later in this book. Initiatives are used to simplify policy assignments. With initiatives, you do not need to assign several policies. You assign one initiative and add the corresponding policies to it.

Initiative assignments

Just like with policies, initiatives need to be assigned to a specific scope in order to be applied. The scope for initiative assignments is identical to a policy assignment's scope.

Policy best practices

When it comes to policy, there are some best practices that you should keep in mind:

- Define policies and initiatives at the management group level. By doing so, you can assign them to all child subscriptions and resource groups without needing to redefine them. If you define policies and initiatives at the subscription level, you can only assign them to this single subscription. So, in short, definitions should be created at the management group level, while assignments can be at the management, subscription, or resource group level.

- As always, before blocking your users from working, you should first test your new policies. You can do so by defining audit policies instead of starting with a deny policy. With the audit effect, you can get a feeling for the impact your policy definition will make. A deny policy could break your DevOps deployment chain and, with an audit effect, you will get an idea of what your policy will do later.

- It is a good idea to create initiative definitions, even if you only want to create a single policy definition. If you have an initiative, you can easily add further policies later if you need to do so.

- All policies within an initiative definition are evaluated when the initiative definition is evaluated. If you have a particular policy you do not want to be evaluated within that context, you should remove it from the definition and assign it individually.

In the preceding sections, you have learned about governance in general, scopes, policies, and locks. In the next section, you will learn how to bring it all together by defining Azure blueprints.

Defining Azure blueprints

Now that you know how to define your Azure hierarchy and how to work with locks and policies, you might want to create a template that is valid for all your subscriptions and for those that are yet to be created as well. With the Azure blueprints service, you get exactly what you need for this purpose. A blueprint, in this case, is a repeatable template that you define once and then use during the creation of all your Azure subscriptions in the future. The good thing here is that you can define organizational sets of rules and automatically apply them to all your subscriptions while accelerating the deployment process at the same time. With Azure Blueprints, you can declaratively deploy Azure resources and artifacts to all your subscriptions, such as the following:

- Role assignments
- Policy assignments
- ARM templates
- Resource groups
- Locks

In the section about management locks in this chapter, I explained that I usually have a core resource group in all of my subscriptions and my customers' subscriptions. These resource groups are usually locked so they are protected from accidental deletion. In larger organizations, you might want to give your developers or specialty departments options for creating their own environments without breaking your rules. No matter what it is, as soon as you want to automate complex deployments of standardized Azure environments, Azure Blueprints is your service of choice!

Blueprint definitions

Azure blueprints are defined by so-called artifacts. An artifact can currently be one of the following:

- **Resource group**: A resource group that is created by a blueprint can be used by other artifacts within the scope of the blueprint. For example, you can create a resource group in a blueprint and then reference an ARM template to this new resource group.

- **Policy assignment**: You can assign an existing policy to a subscription or resource group that a blueprint is assigned to. For example, you can assign the only-European-Azure-locations policy from one of the preceding chapters in this book.

- **Role assignment**: You can assign management access to a subscription that this blueprint is assigned to. For example, you can automatically assign contributor rights to new subscriptions for your infrastructure administrators.

- **ARM template**: With an ARM template, you can declaratively deploy complex Azure environments. ARM templates can be used within the scope of Azure blueprints. For example, you can automatically create a new Log Analytics workspace in a core resource group that is created within the scope of a blueprint.

> **Important Note:**
> A blueprint definition can be saved either to a management group or a subscription. If you create a blueprint definition at the management group level, you can use the blueprint for assignment on all child subscriptions within the scope of this particular management group.

Blueprint publishing

Every new blueprint that is created will initially be in *draft* mode. After finishing all configurations, the blueprint needs to be *published*. When publishing a blueprint, you need to define a *version* string and optional change notes. When additional changes are made to this blueprint, the published version will still exist and changes are done in draft mode, again.

When changing a blueprint (and saving the changes), several versions of the same blueprint will exist to make sure that you can still assign old versions and that published versions are not touched when applying changes to the blueprint.

You can start by creating a new blank blueprint or selecting one of the blueprint examples from the Azure portal. For example, there are blueprint definitions that assign policies that are necessary to address specific NIST SP 800-53 R4 or ISO 27001 controls:

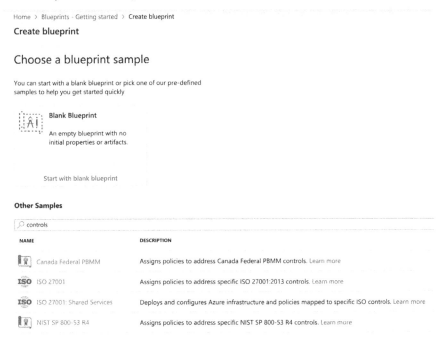

Figure. 2.8 – When creating a blueprint definition, you can choose
one of the predefined sample blueprints

To start creating a blueprint definition, do the following:

1. Navigate to **All Services** -> **Blueprints**.

2. Select **Create**.

3. When the wizard appears, you need to give your blueprint a name and then select the location to save your blueprint definition. In the following screenshot, I decided to save the blueprint in my `Tenant Root Group` to be able to use the blueprint in all subscriptions that are or may later be attached to my Azure AD tenant:

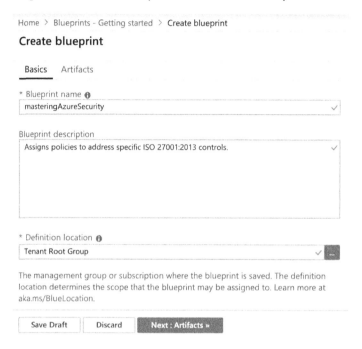

Figure. 2.9 – Creating a blueprint – basic information

I decided to use the `ISO 27001` blueprint sample for this demonstration. On the second tab, the **Artifacts** tab, you can add, remove, or edit artifacts according to your needs. You can save your draft anytime and come back later if you want to change, add, or remove anything:

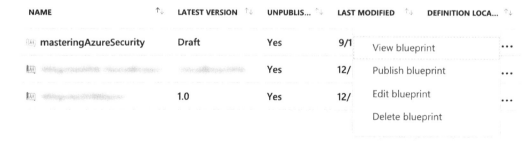

Figure. 2.10 – Context dialog after saving the blueprint in draft mode

4. When you are done, you need to publish your blueprint definition to a new version. The version is basically a custom text field that you need to define. It makes sense to select version numbers so that you can easily iterate through your versions. However, you can use whatever blueprint version names fit your needs. I decided to name the blueprint version 0.1:

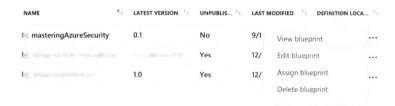

NAME		LATEST VERSION	UNPUBLIS...	LAST MODIFIED	DEFINITION LOCA...	
masteringAzureSecurity		0.1	No	9/1	View blueprint	...
			Yes	12/	Edit blueprint	...
		1.0	Yes	12/	Assign blueprint	...
					Delete blueprint	

Figure. 2.11 – Context dialog after publishing the new blueprint

After publishing your blueprint, the context dialog changes and gives you a new menu option, **Assign blueprint**.

5. You can now assign your new blueprint to any of your existing subscriptions or choose to create a new subscription right from the dialog:

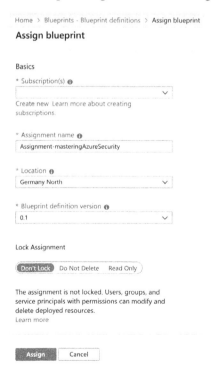

Figure. 2.12 – New blueprint assignment

As soon as you assign your blueprint, the policies you defined in the blueprint definition are applied, and resource groups and resources are created. You can also assign a lock when assigning a blueprint. If you apply a lock during blueprint assignment, you can only remove it when unassigning the blueprint.

> **Important Note:**
> You can assign a management lock when assigning a blueprint to a subscription. However, if you do so, the lock cannot simply be removed by a subscription owner but only when unassigning the blueprint from the subscription.

You need to define a location for your blueprint assignment. This is because blueprints use **Managed Identity (MI)** to deploy the artifacts you define in your blueprint definition, such as resources and resource groups. You can either use a *system-assigned* MI or decide to use a *user-assigned* MI. If you use a system-assigned MI, which is the default, this MI is temporarily granted owner rights on the subscription(s) within the scope of your blueprint assignment. Owner access is needed to make sure that all your artifacts and locks can properly be created and set by the Blueprints service. When the blueprint assignment process is finished, owner access for the system-assigned MI is automatically removed from your subscription(s).

Depending on the artifacts you have defined in your blueprint definition, you might have to define your artifact parameters during the assignment process:

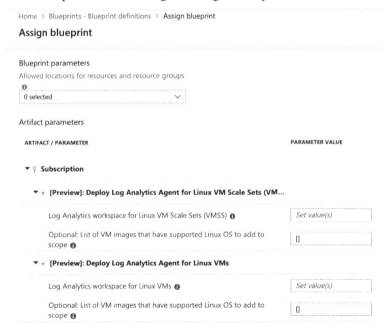

Figure. 2.13 – Artifact parameters are configured during blueprint assignments

In our example, we started with the ISO 27001 blueprint example. This blueprint definition contains several policies, such as policies for restricting resource deployment to only a few Azure regions or for deploying Azure Log Analytics agents to Windows and Linux VMs. All parameters for these policies could have been defined in the blueprint definition already. However, if we had done so, all parameters would always be the same for all subscriptions and could not be defined depending on the subscription you assign a blueprint to. This might be great for corporate restrictions that need to be enforced for every system environment, but it would restrict the blueprint/policy flexibility.

The best practice for this case is to define all parameters that can never be changed in the blueprint definition. For example, this could be useful if there are only certain Azure regions that are permitted for your company's resources. But for Log Analytics, it makes sense to deploy a separate workspace to every Azure region, so as to avoid being charged for cross-region network traffic. This would ideally be defined during blueprint assignment.

Tip

Best Practice: Define artifact parameters that are valid for all your subscriptions in the *blueprint definition*. Define artifact parameters that only fit specific subscriptions during *blueprint assignment*.

Now that you know how to define your governance concepts and how all the features we have today work together, we will take a close look at Azure Resource Graph, an engine that helps you to gather information about all the resources you have created within the scope of your Azure tenant.

Azure Resource Graph

Have you ever tried to get information about all the Azure resources that are deployed outside of Europe? Or what about listing all the Azure VMs across all your subscriptions? In the *Understanding Governance in Azure* section, I mentioned that monitoring is essential for security and that you are clueless if you do not have effective monitoring practices. Now, if you tried to get information such as the information we have discussed when covering **Azure Resource Manager** (**ARM**), you might end up waiting forever. You might not even have the ability to get all the information you need at once.

Azure Resource Graph is a relatively new service that helps you to gather information about all your Azure resources across all your tenants' Azure subscriptions. Sounds great, doesn't it? Well, it is great.

You can think of Azure Resource Graph as a large index database for all your resources that can be queried using **Kusto Query Language** (**KQL**). As soon as you create a new or update an existing resource, ARM notifies Azure Resource Graph of this change and the Azure Resource Graph database is updated. To make sure that there is no notification missed, and in case you update resources outside of ARM, Azure Resource Graph regularly runs a full scan of your resources in addition to receiving the notifications, so that the database is kept current.

In order to be able to use Azure Resource Graph to query your resources, you need to have at least read access to the resources you want to query. In other words, you are presented with results only for the resources that you are allowed to see. So, query results always depend on the account that is currently logged in to the Azure portal, the Azure CLI, PowerShell, or the REST API.

Querying Azure Resource Graph with PowerShell

If you want to use PowerShell to query Azure Resource Graph, follow these steps:

1. Install the `Az.resourcegraph` PowerShell module with the following commands.

    ```
    First, install the PowerShell module for Azure Resource
    Graph:
    install-module Az.resourcegraph
    ```

    Then, import the module into your current PowerShell session:

    ```
    import-module Az.resourcegraph
    ```

2. Make sure that the module was properly installed by using the following PowerShell command:

    ```
    get-command -module Az.resourcegraph
    ```

    You should see the following output:

    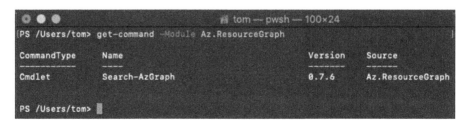

    Figure. 2.14 – The Az.ResourceGraph module was successfully installed and imported

Currently, the Az.ResourceGraph PowerShell module online contains one cmdlet, which is Search-AzGraph. This might be subject to change in the future, so make sure to always use the latest version of the PowerShell module.

You can now start to query Azure Resource Graph with PowerShell. Let's, for example, get a list of all Azure resources that contain the word "core" in their name. We want to limit the output to five results. Now, the interesting thing is that the Search-AzGraph cmdlet already gives you the database column, which is to be queried, so for the query, you only need to define your filter logic.

A KQL query usually looks like this:

```
database |
where <filter logic> |
project columnname1, columname2 |
limit n
```

Since the database name is given by Search-AzGraph, we only need to define the filter logic. So, for the result just described, your PowerShell command, including the query, could be as follows:

```
Search-AzGraph -Query 'project name, type | where name
contains "core" | limit 5'
```

This command will give you up to five results that contain the word core anywhere in the resource name:

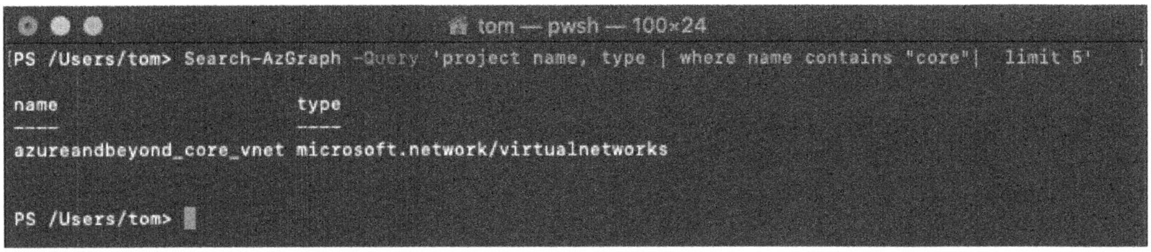

Figure. 2.15 – Your first Azure Resource Graph query result with PowerShell

You've now learned how to use Powershell to query Azure Resource Graph. In the next section, you will learn how to leverage Azure CLI for the same results.

Querying Azure Resource Graph with the Azure CLI

As you might have recognized from the preceding screenshot, I am using PowerShell Core in a macOS Bash terminal. This works absolutely fine, and since I am into both PowerShell and macOS, for me this is a great way to go. However, with the Azure CLI, the Python-based command-line interface that can be run on Windows, macOS, and Linux, you can also easily query Azure Resource Graph. If you have already installed the latest version of the Azure CLI, you just need to interactively log in with the following command:

```
az login
```

You will then be informed that there is a browser window open that you can use to enter your credentials, beat the MFA challenge, and handle all the other security stuff that comes with Azure AD (and which we will address in the next chapter of this book). As soon as you have logged in, the Azure CLI will give you an overview of all the subscriptions that your account has access rights to:

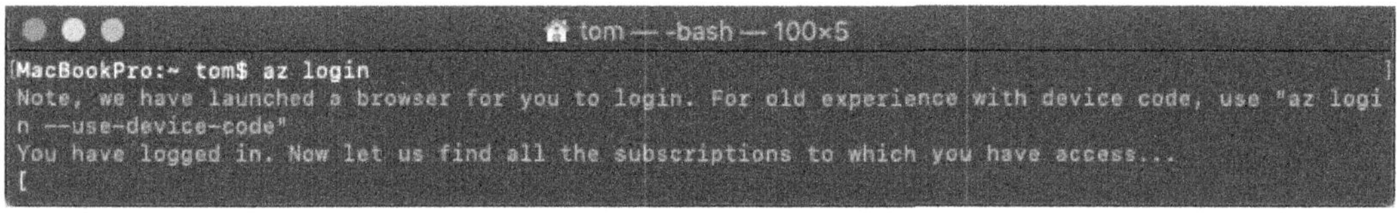

Figure. 2.16 – Azure CLI – interactive login successful

If you now try to get help for `az graph` (which is the starting command to get access to Azure Resource Graph), you will see an error message because the graph extension needs to be added to your Azure CLI environment first:

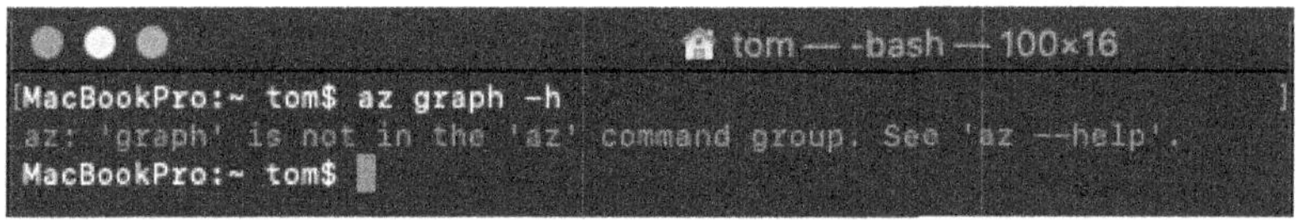

Figure 2.17 – Error message when the Azure Resource Graph extension has not yet been enabled in the Azure CLI

So, let's add the graph extension:

1. Enter the following command into the Bash session:

    ```
    az extension add --name resource-graph
    ```

2. You can now run the same query you have run in PowerShell (but with the Azure CLI syntax):

```
az graph query -q "project name, type | where name
contains 'core' | limit 5"
```

Running this query will give you the following output:

```
● ● ●                          🏠 tom — -bash — 100×8
[MacBookPro:~ tom$ az graph query -q "project name, type | where name contains 'core' | limit 5"    ]
[
  {
    "name": "azureandbeyond_core_vnet",
    "type": "microsoft.network/virtualnetworks"
  }
]
MacBookPro:~ tom$ ▌
```

Figure 2.18 – Your first Azure Resource Graph query result with the Azure CLI

So, the query itself will stay the same. It is only wrapped in the Azure CLI syntax instead of PowerShell.

Advanced queries

Now that you know how to run queries against Azure Resource Graph with the Azure CLI and PowerShell, you may be interested in running some advanced queries, right? So, here you go. The queries you find here can be run in both the Azure CLI and Powershell.

First, let's try to get more information about a resource – not just the name and type, and without limiting the output to a number of results; let's filter for a particular subscription. The query might be as follows:

```
where subscriptionId == 'your subscription ID' and name
contains 'core'
```

The command for the Azure CLI is as follows:

```
az graph query -q "where subscriptionId == 'your
subscription ID' and name contains 'core'"
```

For PowerShell, you enter the following command:

```
Search-AzGraph -Query "where subscriptionId == 'your
subscription ID' and name contains 'core'"
```

You will see, depending on your access rights and the resource type, that the results of your query will now give you a lot of information. A screenshot of the single resource that shows up as the result in my environment, a virtual network, would take up about two pages of this book. The nice thing is that even if there are lots of resources returned by your query, you will get your results in near-real time because you query the Azure Resource Graph database instead of Azure Resource Manager, which would have to "talk" to each and every resource first.

Summary

In this chapter, you have learned why governance is essential for security and what features Azure has to offer to help you in building a governance concept for your company. You've learned how to group and organize subscriptions and resources, how to enforce policies and all the best practices to ensure that you do so effectively and without breaking your system, and how to create consistent and repeatable environments. We know that it is not easy to find a way through this jungle of options, but when you stop, think, plan, act, and repeat, you will be on a good path to finding what fits your needs perfectly.

In the next chapter, you will not only learn how to keep track of access rights and monitor any anomalies in user behavior by learning how to manage cloud identities, but you will also learn about strategies to protect identities and how to reduce the attack surface of privileged accounts.

Questions

1. What are the most important parts of governance?

   A. Policies

   B. Monitoring

   C. Implementation

   D. All of the above

2. What needs to be defined in governance when deployment is in question?

   A. We need to define what can be deployed

   B. We need to define deployment steps

   C. We need to define both what and how

   D. This depends on the deployment method

3. Which feature prevents the accidental removal of resources?

    A. Resource locks

    B. Delete locks

    C. Management locks

4. What is the top level of a group hierarchy?

    A. Tenant

    B. Management group

    C. Subscription

    D. Resource group

5. At which level are Azure Blueprints applied?

    A. Resource

    B. Subscription

    C. Resource group

6. What can we define with Azure Blueprints?

    A. Role assignments

    B. Policy assignments

    C. Both of the above

    D. None of the above

7. What is Azure Resource Graph?

    A. A service to control deployments

    B. A service to gather information

    C. Both of the above

    D. None of the above

3
Managing Cloud Identities

Back in the days when IT security was synonymous with blocking network traffic, life was easy. You could be sure that your physical walls built your perimeter, so you simply needed to protect your borders. However, today, your network endpoints are no longer enough to secure your perimeter. Today, we see an increasing amount of phishing and credential theft attacks against corporate environments. We're in an age where corporate data is moving out of its secure enterprise network environment. It's the age of cloud services such as Office 365, and so traditional security strategies aren't enough to safeguard data as the data is outside secure walls. We need a new approach to add on top of the traditional approach. This new approach is "identity is the new perimeter." This makes identity something we need to protect more than ever before. Of course, this does not mean that we have to do away with the old method of protecting the network, and we'll explore this in *Chapter 4, Network Security*.

In general, to avoid random attacks, you need to raise the bar and make an attack attempt as expensive as possible for an attacker. It's just like protecting your home: if you secure your front door with a higher **resistance class** (**RC**), have grids in front of your windows, an automated lighting system to light up your property, and your neighbor does not, then burglars looking for random targets will most probably not even try to attack your home. This is because an attack attempt against your home would probably be too time consuming, or the probability of being detected is too high; thus, it would be too expensive from an attacker's point of view. This does not work if you are suffering a sophisticated attack that is planned and targeted against your home or identities (there is no absolute security!), but it helps against all the random attack attempts out in the wild.

In this chapter, we will not only cover strategies to protect your identities, but you will also learn how to reduce the attack surface of your privileged accounts. The topics we will cover are the following:

- Exploring passwords and passphrases
- Understanding **multi-factor authentication (MFA)**
- Using Conditional Access
- Introducing **Azure Active Directory (Azure AD)** Identity Protection
- Understanding **role-based access control (RBAC)**
- Protecting admin accounts with Azure AD **Privileged Identity Management (PIM)**
- Hybrid authentication and **Single Sign-On (SSO)**
- Understanding passwordless authentication
- Licensing considerations

Exploring passwords and passphrases

When talking about identity security, there is one principle you always have to keep in mind: *assume breach*. The question is not *whether your accounts are attacked* but *whether you know about it* and *whether you can prevent attackers from being successful*. We can already see that there are many successful attacks against cloud identities every day. There is no single solution for protecting your identities, but you need to leverage a broader toolset to be resilient against identity attacks.

> **Important Note**
> The question is not whether your cloud identities are under attack but whether you can make sure that attackers are not successful.

If we start with passwords, you could say that no one likes them. Well, attackers do, because they often give attackers leverage for a following **identity-focused attack** attempt. Given the fact that people tend to create their passwords based on their life experiences, an attacker generally needs to be good at gathering background information about a specific user to guess their password. This, of course, means some effort on the attacker's side, and this would most probably be executed in a sophisticated attack against a high-value target. You can see that passwords are not a good solution for protecting your accounts.

Furthermore, passwords can lead to **denial of service (DoS)**. In **Active Directory Domain Services (AD DS)** on Windows Server, lots of companies use a respective security policy that will lock out user accounts for a given time (or infinitely) after a given number of failed login attempts. The problem is that authenticated users—that is, users that have been able to log into Active Directory — are able to read this security policy, and they are able to list user accounts from AD. An authenticated user can be any employee (internal attacker), or someone who is trying to attack a company from outside and who was able to get access to a set of login credentials (external attacker). Leveraging PowerShell, an attacker can easily:

- Find out what security policy is in place
- List all user accounts
- Lock all user accounts by trying to log in with incorrect passwords
- Repeat this script every *x* number of minutes.

If someone does so, no one in this directory will be able to log in again, so the company will suffer a DoS. That said, you should *not* implement this lockout policy but monitor login attempts instead, and then make educated decisions if something unusual happens. Keep an eye on your security event logs on Windows servers or the syslog/auth log domain on Linux.

Dictionary attacks and password protection

Dictionary attacks, such as brute-force and password spray attacks, still find success every day. In a dictionary attack, attackers try combinations of usernames and well-known and often-used passwords against an authentication service. The brute-force attack is more noisy and easier to recognize. With brute force, an attacker will try lots of passwords for a single user account, hoping that one of the attacks will be successful. In the backend, you will see lots of failed login attempts, so you can easily react to it. However, a password spray attack is way more sensitive since an attacker will only use a small set of passwords against lots of user accounts. If the attacks are very slow and widely distributed, it is very hard to notice an attack. To avoid successful password spray and brute-force attacks in the cloud and, to be more precise, in Azure AD, there are some easy best practices:

- Encourage your users to use passphrases instead of passwords
- Block passwords or patterns that should not be used in your environment

Currently, you can use passwords or passphrases with up to 256 (!) characters in Azure AD. Even if you were to only use all 26 letters from the alphabet in uppercase and lowercase, this would mean $(2x26)^{256}$ 256 possibilities, which results in a number near infinity.

That said, and knowing that you cannot only use uppercase and lowercase letters, but also numbers and other characters in a passphrase, it makes a whole lot of combinations. You see, you should definitely enable and encourage your users to use passphrases with a lot of letters.

For passwords you do not want to allow in your organization, there is another option you can enable. By default, Microsoft does not allow you to use passwords or password patterns that can be found on password lists and that are known to be used in dictionary attacks. For example, a pattern that is not allowed is your username, or any part of it. In addition to that, it might make sense for your company to avoid passwords that are easily relatable to your enterprise. This could be well-known marketing phrases, corporate abbreviations, and so on. In Azure AD, there is an option to create a custom banned password list that can be used to either audit or enforce the usage of secure passwords. You can even use this custom list to enable password protection for your on-premises Windows Server AD by installing and enabling an on-premises agent.

The custom banned password list can contain up to 1,000 case-sensitive terms between 4 and 16 characters in length. One nice feature is the fact that character substitution such as "e" and "3" or "o" and "0" is considered.

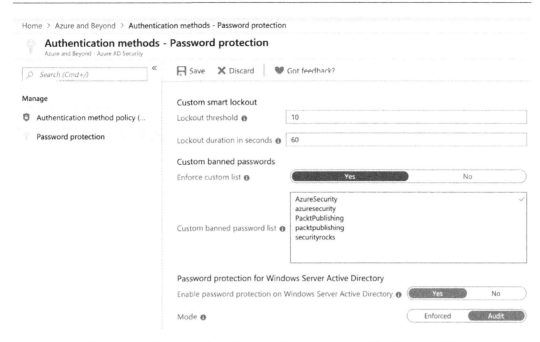

Figure. 3.1 - Configuration of a custom banned password list in Azure AD

In order to configure a custom banned password list, you need to navigate to **Azure Active Directory** -> **Authentication methods** -> **Password protection** in the Azure portal, as seen in *Fig. 3.1*. On that screen, you'll also find configuration options for the **Custom smart lockout** feature. As mentioned before, you might find an on-premises AD security policy forcing accounts to be locked after a given number of failed login attempts. This is kind of an on/off decision and you can easily increment the lockout counter with the same password to force account lockouts. Remember that this is why you should disable such policies in your on-premises AD and monitor login attempts instead.

However, in Azure AD, smart lockout is the feature that combines the best of two worlds: letting users work without blocking them unnecessarily and preventing attackers from guessing your passwords at the same time. To achieve that goal, smart lockout comes with some interesting features:

- Users are not meant to be blocked from working. Smart lockout recognizes attack attempts and login attempts from valid users. Attack attempts are treated differently, so legitimate users are still able to work while attackers are blocked.

- Smart lockout stores the last three bad password hashes. Doing so, you cannot simply use the lockout counter to enforce DoS by using the same bad password several times.

- The default lockout threshold is 10 bad attempts with a lockout duration of 60 seconds. Smart lockout is always on for Azure AD; however, it does not guarantee that legitimate user accounts are never locked out. The service uses familiar versus unfamiliar locations to try to figure out whether a login attempt comes from a bad actor or a genuine user. However, there is still a probability that users will be blocked from logging in. And one important point is that the service does not necessarily protect you from highly sensitive password spray attacks. This is not because the service is bad but because those kinds of attacks can become really difficult to discover.

- Imagine an attacker has a list of nine passwords and they use a widely spread network of bots to attack thousands of user accounts in one custom domain over a time frame of weeks. In that situation, there are some facts to realize:

  The number of login attempts per user account will not exceed the default threshold.

  By using several widely spread host systems to run the attack, it is hard to discover whether a login attempt is valid or malicious. However, Microsoft will also take into account whether a login attempt comes from a known bad IP address or an unfamiliar location.

So, in this scenario, the service will probably not block an attacker. Of course, the nine passwords in the list need to be quite sophisticated to be accepted. However, there is still a probability of an attacker being successful at guessing your passwords.

Now that you know why passwords are not enough to protect your accounts, let's move one step further and see how MFA can give an additional layer of security to your accounts.

Understanding Multi-Factor Authentication (MFA)

There are only a few technical features that protect your accounts more than using MFA. With MFA, it is not enough to know a username and a password; you are also challenged to prove who you are using another authentication factor. With MFA, you generally need to be able to log in with:

- Something you are, such as your user account name or a biometrical attribute

- Something you know, such as a password

- Something you have, such as an additional authentication factor (smartcard, smartphone app, or security key).

Given the fact that an MFA challenge is only triggered after a successful login attempt, it is still reliant on passphrases that are not easy to guess. In other words: if an MFA challenge is triggered, the respective username/password combination has already been successfully validated.

 Microsoft

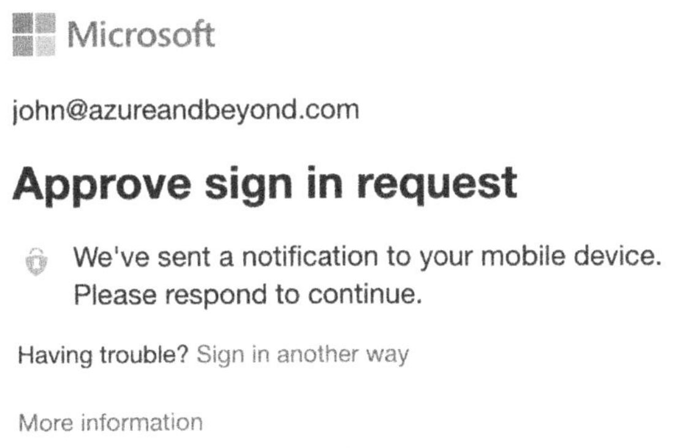

john@azureandbeyond.com

Approve sign in request

We've sent a notification to your mobile device.
Please respond to continue.

Having trouble? Sign in another way

More information

Figure. 3.2 - An MFA challenge is triggered after the user's credentials have successfully been validated

Today, there are several options for using MFA in Azure AD:

- A push message from the Microsoft Authenticator smartphone app
- A **one-time password** (**OTP**) from the Microsoft Authenticator smartphone app
- A text message with an OTP sent to your mobile device
- A phone call to an authentication phone
- A security key or token

If you have set up MFA the right way, you can literally react to all situations with a combination of these options. If you do not have access to mobile data or Wi-Fi, you can use the OTP code from a text message or from your smartphone app. If you leave your smartphone at home, you can get a call to your office phone (or another authentication phone you defined during the configuration process).

> **Important Note**
> Important to note is the fact that you should not use your mobile phone number as your authentication phone because of obvious reasons. If you lose your phone or leave it at home, there won't be many options left.

In *Chapter 2*, *Governance and Security*, you learned about the segregation of duties and the principle of least privilege. Accounts only get the access rights they really need to fulfill a task. However, it is important to prevent being accidentally locked out from your Azure AD environment. So, there is still a need for accounts with higher privileges, such as subscription owner or Global Administrator access. This is why you need to create at least two administrative emergency access accounts. Some of these emergency access or *break glass* accounts need to be protected with MFA, too. Now, a single smartphone does not seem to be a good option for these kinds of accounts, because, according to Murphy's law, something will go wrong; the smartphone's owner is always on holiday, ill, or not available because of other reasons when you need them. A good thing to know is that you can have up to five authentication factors connected to a single account. For example, you could associate three security keys, one smartphone app, and a phone number with one account to make sure that there will always be at least one method you can use to fulfill an MFA challenge.

MFA activation in Azure AD

From an administrator's perspective, activation of MFA in Azure AD is pretty straightforward:

1. In the Azure portal, navigate to **Azure Active Directory** and select the **Users** navigation pane. In the upper-right corner, navigate to •••**More** and then select **Multi-Factor Authentication**, as shown in the following screenshot:

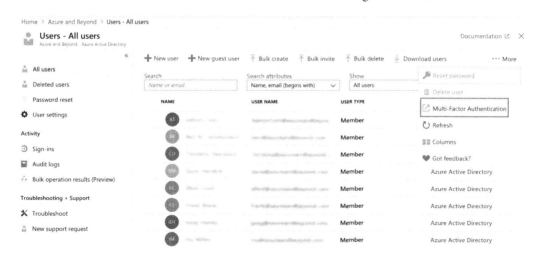

Figure. 3.3 - MFA activation in the Azure portal

You will be redirected to a retro-style portal at the `windowsazure.com` domain, in which you can enable or disable MFA for single users or bulk-update them by selecting several accounts or using a CSV file in the **users** tab.

2. Before you enable MFA for user accounts, first switch from the **users** tab to the **service settings** tab to configure some custom settings for your environment, as shown in the following screenshot:

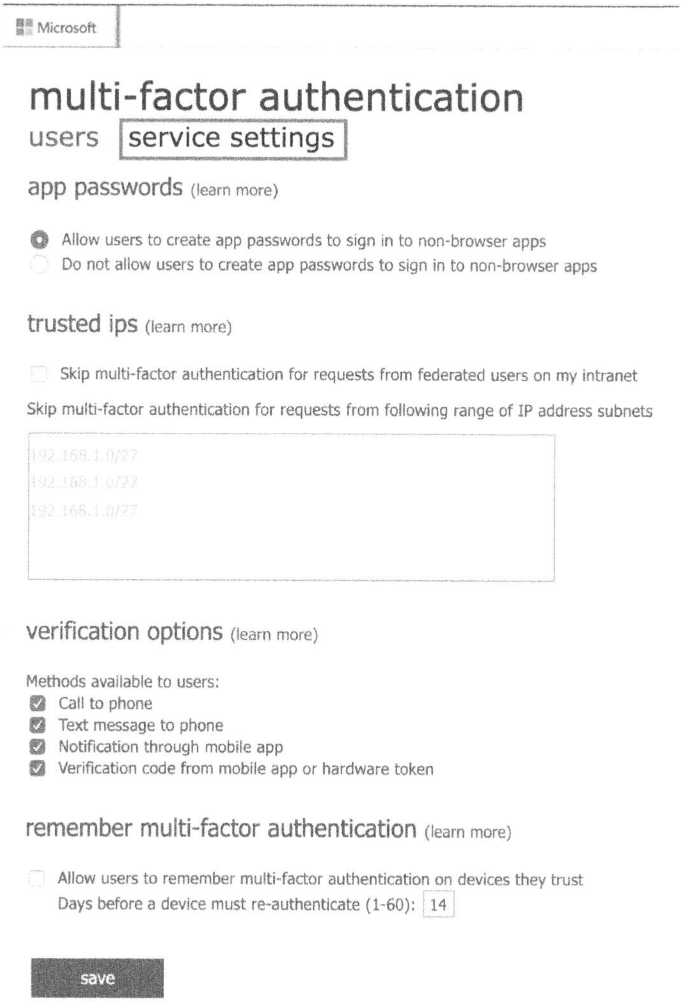

Figure. 3.4 - MFA - service settings

The first option is to allow or disallow users to create app passwords for legacy non-browser apps that do not support MFA. Outlook used to be such an application; however, nowadays, most applications should be able to authenticate with MFA.

You can also define trusted IPs for which you can skip MFA. So, for example, if your users are authenticating from one of your corporate offices and you have defined your external IP range(s) here, you can define that MFA challenges are only triggered when someone wants to authenticate from outside your corporate buildings. You can also enable and disable single verification options if they do not fit your company's needs. The last setting is to allow users to remember MFA for devices they (but not you as a company!) trust. If you enable that option, users are not prompted with an MFA challenge again for a given period of time (between 1 and 60 days) on a particular device.

3. Now, back to enabling user accounts for MFA on the **users** tab. When you click the **Enable** link on the right side after selecting one or several user accounts, you are prompted to read the online deployment guide and then click on **enable multi-factor auth**. That's all from an administrator's point of view. Pretty easy? Indeed.

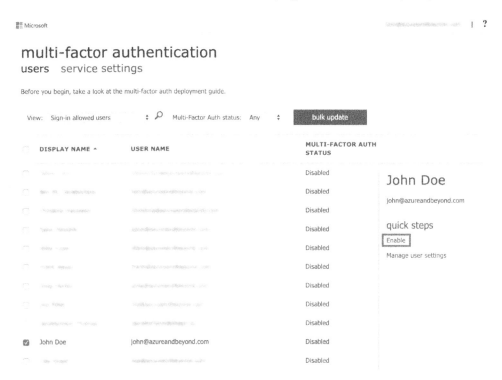

Figure. 3.5 - Enabling MFA for one or several user accounts

The MFA-activated user has to configure all individual settings after the next login attempt. Telephone numbers for the account are taken from the information that is already stored in Azure AD. However, the user can update these numbers in the wizard that appears after the next logon.

MFA activation from a user's perspective

After enforcing MFA for John, a new window will appear after his next successful login, telling him that his organization needs more information to protect his account, as shown in the following screenshot:

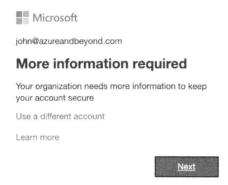

Figure. 3.6 - New window at the first login after MFA activation

John now only has two options: **Use a different account** to log in or click **Next** to proceed through the MFA activation process. That said, you should inform your users before activating MFA to let them know what's going to happen and to reduce the amount of support tickets required!

Let's look at what happens if John decides to complete the process:

John decides to proceed and clicks the **Next** button. On the following screen, he can decide which is going to be his primary authentication option. John's office phone number is already filled from the information stored in his Azure AD user account, and he cannot change it. The authentication phone number, however, can be individually configured.

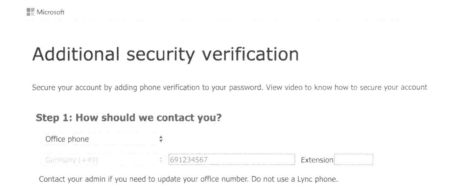

Figure. 3.7 - Office phone numbers cannot be individually changed but are filled from the values stored in the Azure AD user account

If John decides to use the authentication phone as his primary MFA option, he has to configure the number and then decide whether he wants to receive a phone call or a text message containing an OTP:

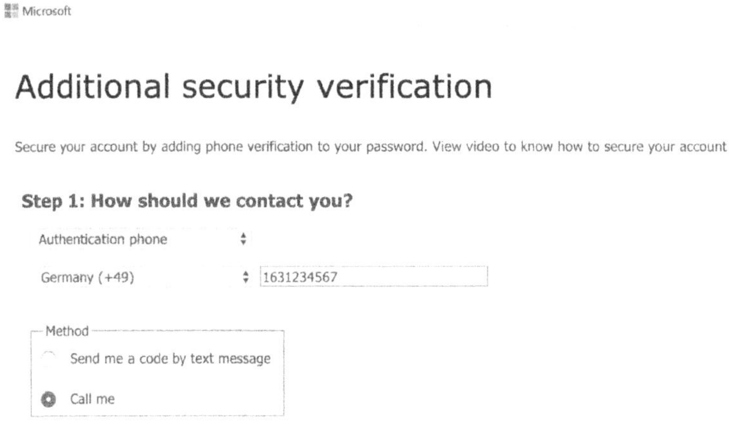

Figure. 3.8 - Authentication phone - individually configure the number and select the contact method

The third option is for John to use the Microsoft Authenticator app, which is available for all major smartphone operating systems in their respective app store. Here, again, he has two options to select from: either being informed by a push notification or using the verification code from the app, which is an OTP that changes every 30 seconds.

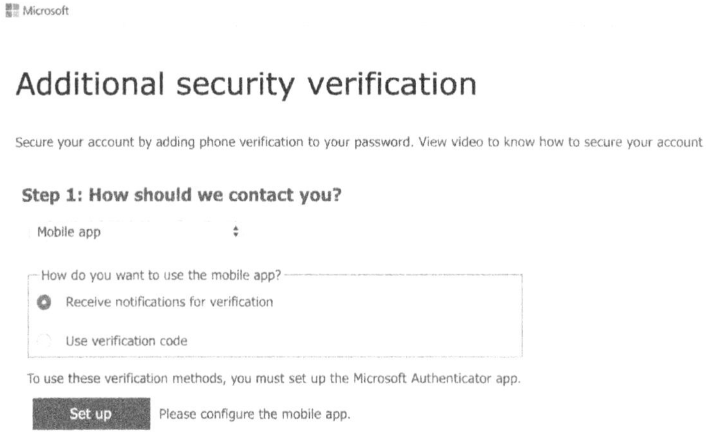

Figure. 3.9 - Mobile app - select the primary MFA verification option

John decides to use the mobile app and so has to click on the **Set up** button. He has already installed the Microsoft Authenticator app on his smartphone, so he can now easily proceed. A new window opens that shows John a **Quick Response (QR)** code to scan with the mobile app, as shown in the following screenshot:

Figure. 3.10 - Mobile app configuration window

In his app, John clicks the + symbol and selects the option to add a new **work or school account**. With the QR code scanner that opens in the smartphone app, John scans the code from his screen and will immediately find his account added to the app's account list, as shown in the following screenshot:

Figure. 3.11 - John's account has been added to the account list in his smartphone app

On his computer, John clicks **Next** so the app and the backend service are synchronized. The **configure mobile app** window will disappear again and John is then able to click the **Next** button. A push notification to the smartphone app is triggered, which can then be approved or declined, as shown in the following screenshot:

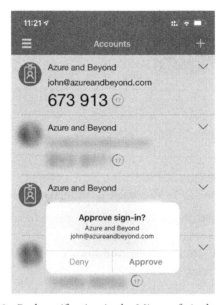

Figure. 3.12 - Push notification in the Microsoft Authenticator app

Next, John is asked to enter his authentication phone number so Microsoft can make sure that John can authenticate logins even when he loses access to the mobile app.

Step 4 then presents John with the app password he needs to use instead of his own user account password. In applications that do not support phone-based MFA today, this password is only shown once, so users need to copy and store it so it can be used when needed. If the app password is not stored safely, users can create new app passwords later, but then again, the respective password is only shown once during creation. After that, the MFA configuration is finished, and John will be logged off. When he logs on again, John will have to accept the MFA challenge.

MFA, in combination with strong passwords, can protect accounts from more than 95% of attacks, and given the fact that Azure MFA can be used free of charge in the default configuration, there is no reason not to enable it.

Now that you know how to configure MFA from an administrator's and a user's perspective, let's move one step further and learn how conditional access can be used to fine-tune the MFA process according to your company's business needs.

Using Conditional Access

MFA, the feature we discussed in the previous section, is the perfect option for better protecting your cloud identities. But it is still kind of an on/off decision. Either you activate a user account for MFA or you don't. Wouldn't it be great to dynamically react to authentication attempts and then decide whether an MFA challenge is needed? With **Conditional Access**, there is a feature that enables us to define authentication conditions that require more or fewer challenges in the authentication process.

Conditional Access gives customers a broad variety of options to include or exclude in a policy. For example, you could enforce the usage of MFA for specified directory roles, such as Azure AD Global Administrators, and in addition to that, require that the login is performed on a corporate-owned device. Or, you could exclude your "normal" Office 365 workers from being challenged by MFA, but only if they are working from a corporate office. As soon as one of them tries to log in from a train station, mobile device, home office, and so on, an MFA challenge is triggered. You see, there are lots of options, and we'll cover them in this section.

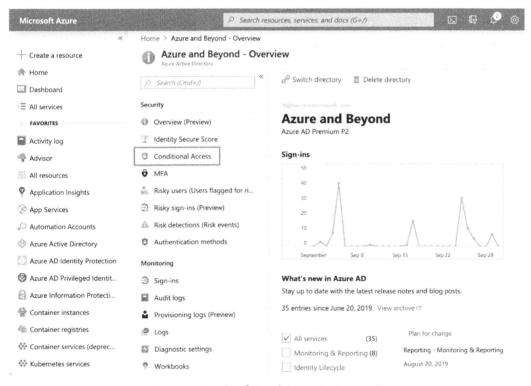

Figure. 3.13 - Conditional Access in Azure AD

You'll find all Conditional Access-related settings in the Azure portal under **Azure Active Directory** > **Conditional Access**:

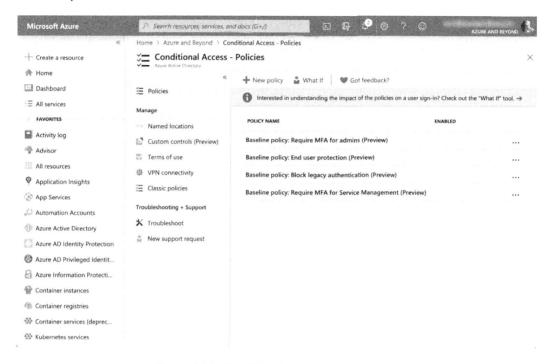

Figure. 3.14 - Conditional Access overview page

The main section that appears now is the **Policies** section. Conditional Access policies define and enforce the complexity of authentication based on several conditions. Policies can depend on locations from which authentications come, user and sign-in risk, devices, applications, or a combination of all of these. You can use Conditional Access policies to decide when and for whom access to your cloud environment will be allowed or blocked. So, by using Conditional Access policies, you can always make sure to apply the right amount of security enforcements when they are needed to keep your environment secure, and not to challenge your users unnecessarily when not needed.

Before we take a deeper look at how to define all those conditions in a Conditional Access policy, let's first have a look at named locations that can be used within these policies.

Named locations

There is a management area to define custom settings you can use in your Conditional Access policies. The first area to mention is **Named locations**. For **Named locations**, there are two different options to click. The first option is **Configure MFA trusted IPs**, which will redirect you to the **Services** settings in the legacy portal you already know from the previous section. You can use this option to define IP address ranges that should always be excluded from MFA challenges.

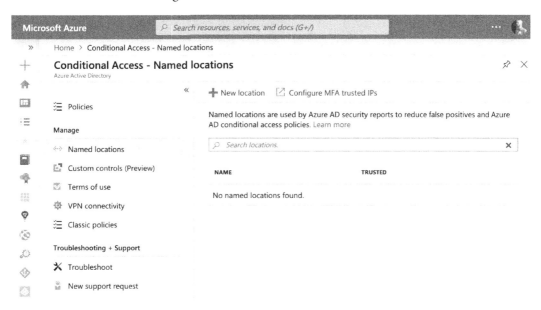

Figure. 3.15 - Conditional access - named locations

The second option is **+ New location**, with which you can define IP ranges, and even countries and geographical regions, to use them for custom Conditional Access policies. If you select **Mark as trusted location** for an IP range, a user's sign-in risk is lowered when an authentication request comes from there.

Figure. 3.16 - Creating a trusted named location

Sign-in risks are important for Azure AD Identity Protection, the feature we look into in the *Introducing Azure AD Identity Protection* section.

Custom controls

With *custom controls*, you can redirect your users during the authentication process to an external compatible service to satisfy further authentication requirements outside of Azure AD. The user's browser window is redirected to a third-party service, where the user needs to perform any further authentication requirements before being granted access to their cloud resources. Custom controls depend on the third-party application. For example, you could integrate a third-party MFA provider into your authentication workflow instead of relying on the Azure AD MFA service.

Terms of use

You can define custom terms of use that need to be accepted before users are allowed to access certain cloud applications. For example, you could allow users to use their own devices to access your environment, but only if they accept your terms of use.

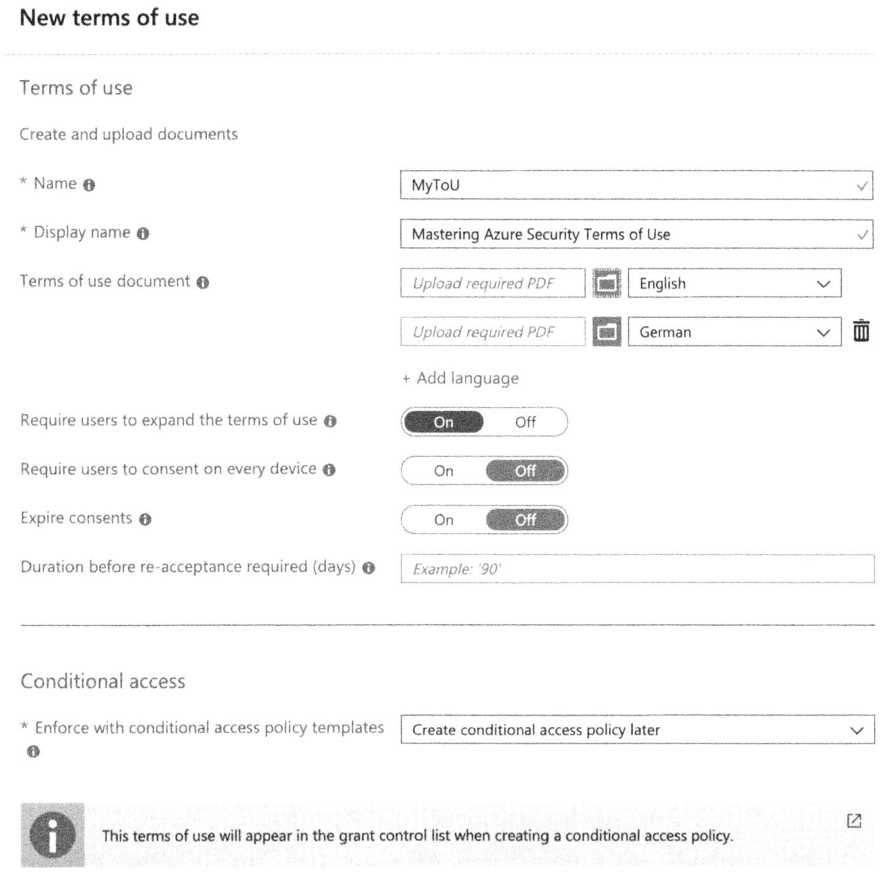

Figure. 3.17 - Terms of use

To configure your custom terms of use, you need to upload one PDF for every language you want to create them for. After saving, the terms of use will appear in the grant control list when creating a new Conditional Access policy.

Conditional Access policies

As mentioned before, Conditional Access policies help you to always apply the right amount of security for every authentication situation, without unnecessarily blocking or challenging your users when not needed. They can be seen as is, then.

Conditional Access policies consist of *assignments* and *access controls*. Assignments define who will be impacted by this Conditional Access policy and in which situation. Access controls define whether access is blocked or granted, and if it's granted, on which conditions.

Assignments

In the **Assignments** section, you can select users and groups, cloud apps or user actions, and conditions to include or exclude in a Conditional Access policy, as shown in the following screenshot:

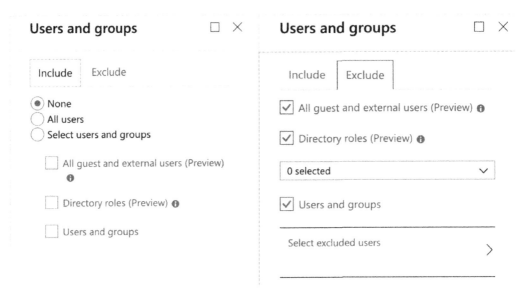

Figure. 3.18 - Users and groups - select which users and groups are to be included
or excluded in a Conditional Access policy

You can choose to **Include** or **Exclude None**, **All users**, or a defined subset of users and groups in a Conditional Access policy. You can also select to exclude all guest and external users, directory roles (such as Global Administrators), or a defined subset of users and groups in your Conditional Access policy.

> **Important Note**
>
> When selecting all users and then blocking access with this policy, this will also affect all your administrator accounts. That said, you could lock yourself out when activating this policy. It is recommended to apply a policy to a small set of users first to make sure it behaves as expected!

You can also **Include** or **Exclude** cloud applications or user actions in the Conditional Access policy. Again, you can select **None, All apps,** or selected apps to be included, or define selected apps to be exempted from the policy.

> **Important Note**
>
> When selecting all cloud apps to be included in your policy, this will also affect the Azure portal. Make sure not to lock yourself out by only activating the policy to a small set of users first, so you can make sure that it behaves as expected!

In the **User actions** section, you can select whether this policy affects the registration of security information for your users. That means that the policy is active for users when proceeding through the MFA registration process.

Conditions to be included in your assignments are sign-in risk, device platforms, locations, client apps, and device state. Sign-in risk is calculated by Azure AD Identity Protection. You can select the sign-in risk level this policy will apply to from **No risk/Low/Medium/High**. Device platforms can be included or excluded. You can select to include any device platform in your policy, or to include or exclude one or several of the following:

- Android
- iOS
- Windows Phone
- Windows
- macOS

You can include any location or select to include or exclude all trusted locations, or selected locations you have already defined in one of the preceding steps.

Client apps to include can either be a browser, or mobile apps and desktop clients, including modern authentication clients, Exchange ActiveSync clients, or other clients (older office clients or other mail protocols).

You can either include all device states in a policy, or exclude devices that are hybrid Azure AD joined or marked as compliant in Intune.

Access controls

In the **Access controls** section, you define whether you want to block or grant access to your environment depending on the selection you made before. If you want to grant access, you can either grant it without any condition or you can require one or all of the following controls to be enforced:

- **Require multi-factor authentication**: When the conditions you defined in the policy are met, user access is granted when the user responds to the MFA challenge.

- **Require device to be marked as compliant**: In Intune, you can define device compliance policies. For example, you can mark a device as compliant only when it is corporate owned and currently patched.

- **Require hybrid Azure AD joined device**: Devices that are hybrid Azure AD joined are owned by an organization. They exist in the cloud and on-premises, which means that they are joined to both Windows Server AD and Azure AD.

- **Require approved client app**: Access is only granted if one of the approved client apps is used to access corporate information. Today, an approved client app can be one out of more than 25 apps related to Microsoft 365, including, but not limited to, Microsoft Azure Information Protection, Microsoft Excel, Microsoft Edge, Microsoft Intune Managed Browser, Microsoft Teams, and Microsoft Outlook.

- **Require app protection policy**: You can use Intune to define an app protection policy for Microsoft Cortana, Microsoft Outlook, Microsoft OneDrive, and Microsoft Planner. With this setting, you can enforce that an app protection policy is present before granting access to corporate information, as illustrated in the following screenshot:

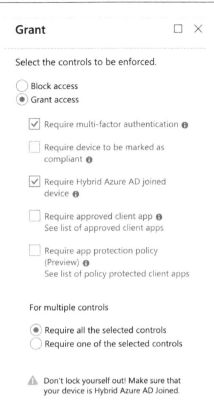

Figure. 3.19 - Conditions for granting access using Conditional Access

Now that you know how to configure Conditional Access policies in theory, let's go a step further and try to define settings for some behaviors.

For example, you could create a policy that blocks access for all devices that are not hybrid Azure AD joined. However, this policy should not affect users that are members of a particular group of administrators. A policy that would fit your needs could include the following:

1. Include all users and exclude the particular group of administrators.

2. Exclude devices that are hybrid Azure AD joined.

3. Block access.

You might also want to enforce MFA when authentication attempts are not coming from a trusted location or if users are not using corporate-owned devices. This policy would:

1. Include all users.

2. Include all locations and exclude all trusted locations.

3.   Grant access and require MFA.

> **Important Note**
> It is best practice not to include all users without exception in your Conditional Access policies. This is because you would risk locking yourself out of your cloud environment.

Your organization might enforce your users to proceed through the MFA enrollment from their office. That way, your organization can make sure that even if a user's credentials have been leaked, an attacker would need to be within your network perimeter to configure MFA. A Conditional Access policy to enforce that might be configured like this:

1.   Include all users and exclude privileged roles or a particular user group containing administrative accounts.

2.   Activate the **Register security information** user action.

3.   Include a selected location that defines your office location.

4.   Block access.

With Conditional Access, you can granularly define when and how access to your cloud environment is granted or declined. During the course of this topic, we have already touched on Azure AD Identity Protection. Now, let's move on to the next section, in which you will learn what Azure AD Identity Protection actually is and how you can use it.

Introducing Azure AD Identity Protection

As already mentioned, an important goal in terms of security is to make attack attempts as expensive as possible for an attacker. That said, it is important to raise the bar and have several complementing technologies in place that add extra value to your security posture. On the other hand, you want to make sure not to block legitimate user authentications so you do not negatively affect your users' login experience. Microsoft has been protecting cloud identities for more than 10 years now, and with Azure AD Identity Protection, they let you protect identities using their protection systems.

Stealing the credentials of user accounts, even if they are not highly privileged, has always been a good way of gaining access to corporate resources. Over the years, attackers have learned to leverage third-party breaches or highly sophisticated phishing attacks to get hold of corporate credentials. Even if attackers gain access to low-privileged user accounts, as soon as they do, it is relatively easy for them to elevate their level of privilege or gain access to important corporate resources through lateral movement.

So, what we need to do is the following:

- Protect all identities at all levels of privilege

- Prevent compromised identities from accessing corporate resources

Now, the second step is the more difficult one because you first need to find out whether an identity is compromised. This is when Azure AD Identity Protection comes into play.

Azure AD Identity Protection at a glance

Adaptive machine learning algorithms and heuristics are what Azure AD utilizes when determining anomalies and suspicious behavior during the authentication of user accounts. With this data, Azure AD Identity Protection can generate reports and alerts that enable customers to evaluate recent logons. Furthermore, Azure AD Identity Protection can calculate user and sign-in risk levels that can be used in risk-based Conditional Access policies. For example, you can decide to enforce the usage of MFA when a login attempt's risk level is calculated as medium or above, or to block a sign-in attempt based on the risk calculation.

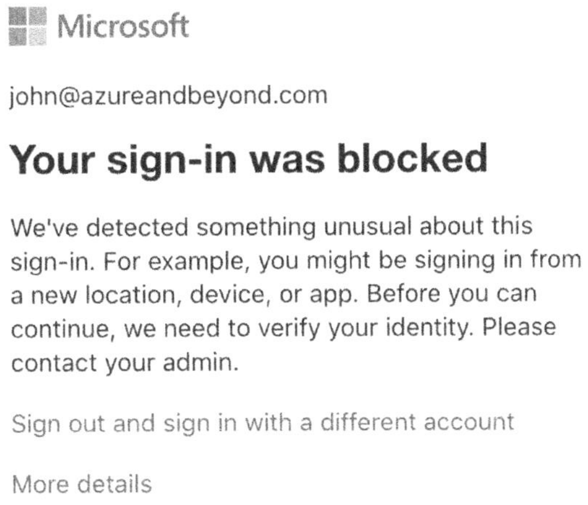

john@azureandbeyond.com

Your sign-in was blocked

We've detected something unusual about this sign-in. For example, you might be signing in from a new location, device, or app. Before you can continue, we need to verify your identity. Please contact your admin.

Sign out and sign in with a different account

More details

Figure. 3.20 - A sign-in was blocked by Azure AD Identity Protection

In the preceding screenshot, you see that a sign-in was blocked because the user's identity could not be verified. This is because John did not have MFA configured before this suspicious sign-in activity was detected. Of course, the person trying to log on and being blocked now is not able to configure MFA at this stage because that would enable attackers to configure the service according to their needs.

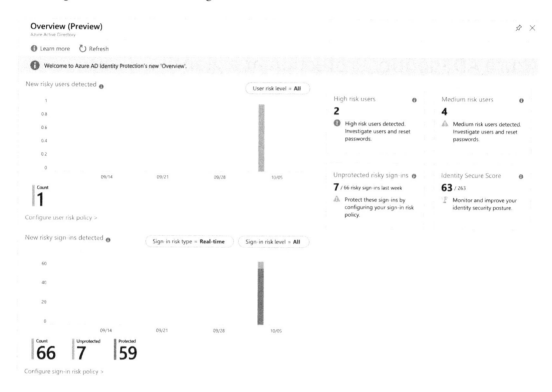

Figure. 3.21 - Azure AD Identity Protection Overview dashboard

Azure AD uses several types of risk detection in realtime (5-10 minutes) and offline (2-4 hours). As soon as there has been a risk detection related to an account sign-in, this detection is added to a logical concept called *risky sign-ins*. A risky sign-in indicates a sign-in attempt that might have been performed by an attacker and not the legitimate account owner. Based on those detections, the probability that the sign-in has been performed by a bad actor is calculated and is reflected in the *sign-in risk level*. You can use the sign-in risk level (**Low**, **Medium**, **High**) to define a *sign-in risk policy*. The sign-in risk policy is an automated response depending on the specified sign-in risk level that is used to either block access to your resources or to require a user to pass an MFA challenge before being granted access to your corporate environment.

Besides the sign-in risk, Azure AD also detects the probability that a user account has been compromised. This behavior is called *user risk detection*. All risk detections that have been detected for a user and that have not been resolved are known as *active risk detections*. All active risk detections that are associated with a user define the user risk. Based on the user risk, Azure AD calculates the probability (**Low**, **Medium**, **High**) that the user account has been compromised. This probability is known as the *user risk level*. For example, if a risky sign-in is detected and the MFA challenge is passed, there is no active risk detection for this user. Thus, in this case, the user risk level will stay low. You can define a *user risk policy* as an automated response for a specific user risk level. With this policy, you can either block access to corporate resources or enforce a password change to get the user back to a clean state.

Risk detection

In Azure AD, there currently are six different types of risk detection:

1. **Users with leaked credentials:** Leaked credentials occur due to mass credential theft by cybercriminals followed by public posting of these credentials, particularly on the dark web. Microsoft actively monitors such channels and compares the leaked username and password pairings against existing users, and identifies accounts that have leaked credentials.

2. **Sign-ins from anonymous IP addresses:** Anonymous IP addresses are used by people who want to mask their device's real IP address. There can be a number of reasons that lead to the use of such IP addresses, some of them malicious. Microsoft checks incoming sign-ins from IP addresses that have previously been identified as anonymous IP addresses.

3. **Impossible travel to atypical locations** are sign-ins from geographically distant locations. At least one location needs to be an atypical location based on the user's sign-in behavior. For example, the user is on his or her first business trip to the US and logs in from there. In addition to that, the underlying machine learning algorithm considers the time between the sign-ins and the time it would have taken the user to travel from one location to the other. Microsoft tries to ignore obvious false-positives, such as **virtual private networks (VPNs)** between locations, or locations that have been known as familiar for other user accounts within the same organization. This risk detection type needs 14 days of analyzing user behavior before being able to calculate the risk for a user account.

4. **Sign-ins from infected devices:** This method of risk detection depends on Microsoft keeping track of IP addresses that are known to communicate with bot servers. Microsoft matches all IP addresses connecting to the service against these known rogue IPs to determine whether there are sign-ins from infected devices. This type of risk detection also targets simple attack methods such as password spray attacks.

5. **Sign-ins from IP addresses with suspicious activity:** In this method of detection, Microsoft examines IPs for signs of suspicious activity. The main indicator is when an IP address has a large number of failed sign-ins in a relatively short period of time. This can be an indication of a bad actor who is trying to guess passwords using simple attack methods such as brute-force or password spray attacks.

6. **Sign-ins from unfamiliar locations:** This method of risk detection involves Microsoft maintaining a historical record of the IP addresses used by users regularly. The system detects whether a request is coming from an IP address that has not been used before. The system needs at least 30 days to create a useable history of familiar and unfamiliar locations.

Creating a sign-in risk or user risk policy

Policy creation is the easiest part of Azure AD Conditional Access. In order to create a sign-in risk policy, you just need to navigate to **Azure AD Identity Protection** -> **Sign-in risk policy** in the Azure portal. There, you define conditions (**Sign-in risk** level - **Low** and above, **Medium** and above, or **High**), access controls (block access or challenge the user with MFA), and select for which user or group you want to enable the policy. That's it.

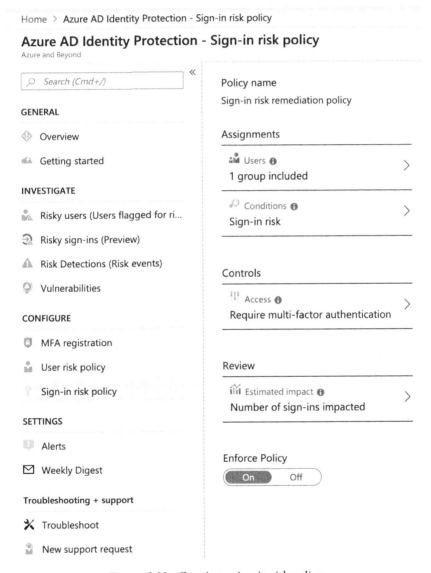

Figure. 3.22 - Creating a sign-in risk policy

For a new user risk policy, you navigate to **Azure AD Identity Protection** -> **User risk policy** and define the respective parameters. The difference from a sign-in risk policy is that you can either block access or enforce a password change for a risky user.

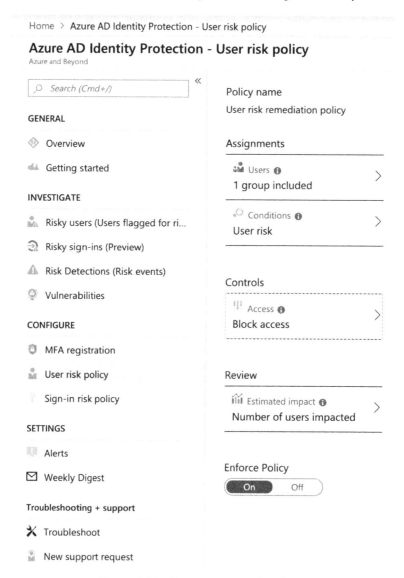

Figure. 3.23 - Creating a user risk policy

Now you know how Azure AD Identity Protection works and how you can use calculated user and sign-in risk levels to protect your accounts. Now, we will move forward and focus on privileged user accounts.

Understanding RBAC

In *Chapter 2, Governance and Security*, we mentioned security principles such as segregation of duties and the principle of least privilege. With RBAC, we have the technical feature to implement these principles in Azure AD. RBAC is the way to manage access to all Azure resources, but also to Azure AD and Office 365.

As already discussed, Azure offers several levels of scope that can be used to grant access rights to accounts. Furthermore, there are several roles, such as **Owner**, **Azure Sentinel Contributor**, or **Reader**, as can be seen in the following screenshot:

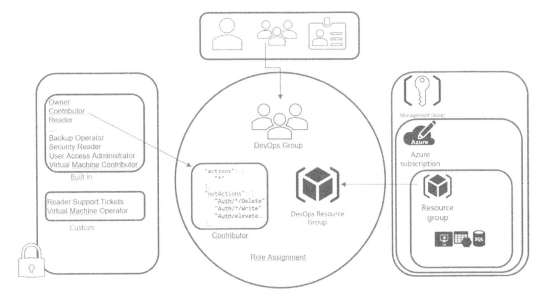

Figure. 3.24 - RBAC role assignment in Microsoft Azure

You need three different entities to create a role assignment:

- A security principal, which can be either one of users, groups, or service principals.

- A role, which describes a set of management rights. For example, the contributor role contains all actions, except authorization-related rights. So, a contributor may manage all aspects at a given scope without being able to grant access to resources.

- A scope to set the access rights, starting from the management group level down to single resources.

If those three come together, this is what we call an RBAC role assignment.

Important Note

You need to be granted `Microsoft.Authorization/` `roleAssignments/write` and `Microsoft.Authorization/` `roleAssignments/delete` rights in order to be able to create or delete role assignments. These rights are, by default, granted to the RBAC roles User Access Administrator and Owner.

You can edit role assignments at all management scopes of Azure. It is important to know that role assignments are inherited top to bottom. This means that if you configure a role assignment at a resource group level, the access rights are also valid on all resources within this particular resource group; and if you configure a role assignment at a management group level, it is inherited to all subscriptions, resource groups, and resources within that scope.

In the Azure portal, there is the **Access Control (IAM)** blade that is used to manage all aspects of RBAC. You can check access for particular accounts, find out explicit and inherited roles and deny assignments, and find out which built-in or custom roles exist for the given scope.

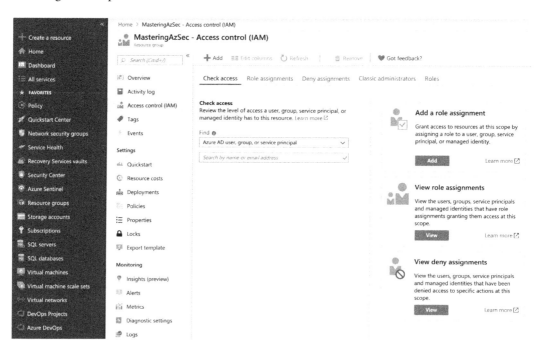

Figure. 3.25 - RBAC management blade in the Azure portal

To create a new role assignment, you need to click **+ Add** and then select **Add role assignment**.

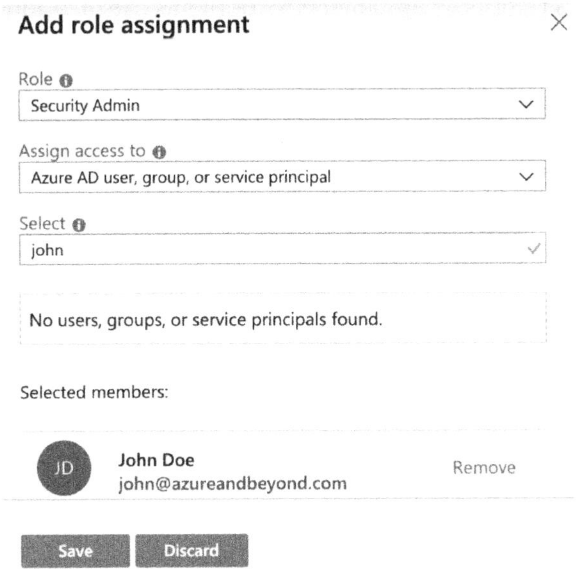

Figure. 3.26 - Adding a role assignment

You then select the role and security principal you want to grant access, and then save your selection. Done.

RBAC is pretty straightforward to implement, but can be way more challenging when planning for access rights in your environment. This is why you should already plan for RBAC roles when defining your governance concept.

> **Important Note**
>
> Define the RBAC roles you need in your environment when creating your governance concept. Doing so, you will have a good overview of which access rights (roles) you need and who (which security principal) you need to grant access to. That said, it will be much easier to create your role assignments later.

In the following section, we will show you how to create custom RBAC roles so you can more granularly use roles according to your needs.

Creating custom RBAC roles

Custom RBAC roles are used whenever built-in roles do not entirely fit your company's needs regarding access rights to your cloud environments. As mentioned before, a role is basically a set of management rights that then are applied to users or groups in a role assignment. There is a difference between *custom Azure AD RBAC roles* and *custom RBAC roles for Azure resources*. If you want to create a custom Azure AD RBAC role, you need to go through the following steps:

1. Navigate to **Azure Active Directory** -> **Roles and administrators** and then click the + **New custom role** button in the Azure portal, as shown in the following screenshot:

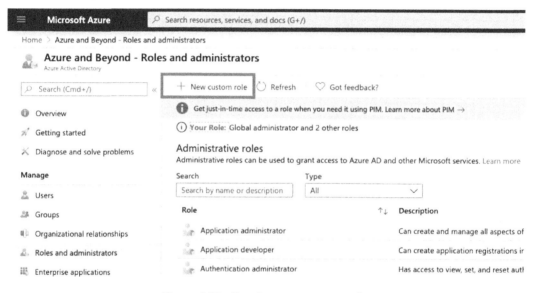

Figure. 3.27 - Creating a new custom role

2. Enter a **Name** and, optionally, a **Description** for your custom role. You can decide either to **Start from scratch**, or to **Clone from a custom role** to continue with your custom role creation. In the following example, we decide to **Start from scratch**:

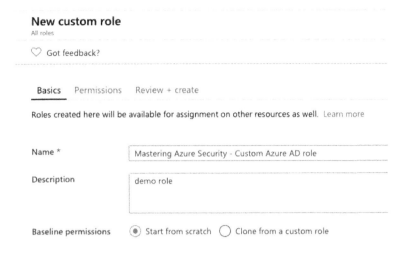

Figure. 3.28 - Defining basic information

3. On the **Permissions** tab, you select all permissions that you later want to grant to your identity.

4. On the **Review + create** tab, you can finally confirm your settings, and by clicking the **Create** button, your custom Azure AD RBAC role is created, as illustrated in the following screenshot:

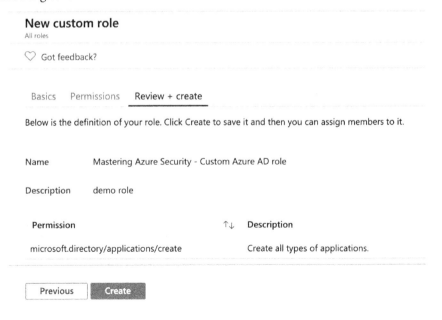

Figure. 3.29 - Reviewing and creating your custom Azure AD RBAC role

The creation of custom RBAC roles for Azure resources cannot be done in the Azure portal. You need to use PowerShell, the Azure **command-line interface (CLI),** or the Azure **representational state transfer (REST)** API. In this example, we will create a custom RBAC role with PowerShell.

To create a custom RBAC role, you need to define which resource operations per resource provider have to be allowed to meet your goals. Therefore, you should initially find out which resource provider operations exist. You can do so by using the `Get-AzProviderOperation` cmdlet, as shown in the following code block:

```
Get-AzProviderOperation <operation> | FT OperationName,
Operation, Description -autosize
```

For example, if you want to find all resource provider operations for the `Microsoft.Compute/VirtualMachines/*` resource provider, the command and the result could look like this:

Figure. 3.30 - Resource provider operations for Azure VMs

The resource provider operations that are listed in the preceding screenshot are all actions related to **virtual machines (VMs)** to which you can grant access to users, groups, or service principals. If you want to know which resource provider operations are tied to a specific RBAC role, you can find this out with the following command:

```
(Get-AzRoleDefinition <role name>).actions
```

For example, if you want to know which actions are allowed for the Virtual Machine Contributor RBAC role, the command would be as follows:

```
(Get-AzRoleDefinition "Virtual Machine Contributor").actions
```

When you know which resource provider operations exist, you can start creating your custom RBAC role. Again, you can start by creating a new role from scratch or by using an existing role as a template to alter according to your needs. You will find examples for creating custom RBAC roles for Azure resources in the GitHub repository belonging to this book.

Now that you have learned what RBAC is and how you can leverage it, we will give you an introduction to **Azure AD Privileged Identity Management (Azure AD PIM)**, another service focused on protecting privileged user accounts. Let's move on!

Protecting admin accounts with Azure AD PIM

In *Chapter 2, Governance and Security*, we discussed the fact that we often see customer environments in which administrators have a huge set of privileges they do not necessarily need. We also discussed **Separation of Duties (SoD)** and the fact that no one should have more privileges than ever needed for doing a particular job. Now, what if you could even reduce that set of access rights to a particular point in time or time range? Or what if you need an approval process for granting privileged access? Maybe you want to monitor the usage of privileged roles or want to decide whether a person still needs privileged access rights?

Azure AD PIM is a service that offers several features that help you further protect privileged accounts, some of which are the following:

- **Just-in-time** and **time-bound** privileged access
- **Approval** to activate privileged roles
- **Access reviews** to ensure that roles are still needed
- Enforcing **MFA** for role activation

With Azure AD PIM, you can—but do not need to—infinitely grant access rights to privileged users; you make them "eligible" for requesting access rights. So, users are only granted access rights when they really need them. Access can be either approved automatically after a user requests access or by manual approval. The nice thing is, you can cover both Azure AD and Azure resource roles with Azure AD PIM.

> **Tip**
> Make sure you have enforced the principle of least privilege in your
> organization before starting with PIM.

Enabling PIM

Before using PIM, you have to enable the service for your directory. You can do so by
signing in to the Azure portal as a Global Administrator of your directory and then
navigating to **Azure AD Privileged Identity Management**. Once there, you will find the
option **Consent to PIM**, as shown in the following screenshot:

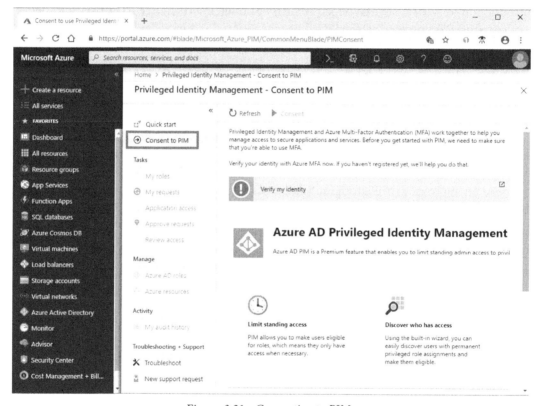

Figure. 3.31 - Consenting to PIM

You then click on **Verify my identity** to verify your identity with MFA. If you haven't
already done so, you will be asked to activate MFA for your account, as covered in the
Understanding Multi-factor Authentication (MFA) section in this chapter. Once your
identity has been verified, you can click the **Consent** button and confirm the dialog by
clicking **Yes**, as shown in the following screenshot:

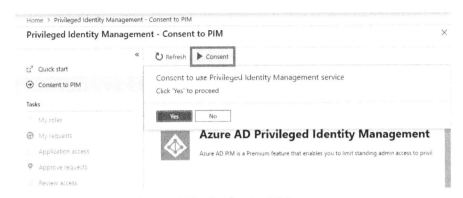

Figure. 3.32 - Confirming PIM consent

Now that you have activated PIM for your directory, you need to sign up to PIM to manage your Azure AD roles. You do so by navigating to the **Azure AD roles** section of the Azure AD PIM dashboard and clicking on **sign up**. Once sign-up completes, the Azure AD options will be enabled.

Managing Azure AD roles in PIM

In the **Azure AD roles** view, you can manage PIM behavior for all Azure AD roles and also have access to Azure AD role-related tasks such as access reviews, approvals, or your own roles and access requests, as shown in the following screenshot:

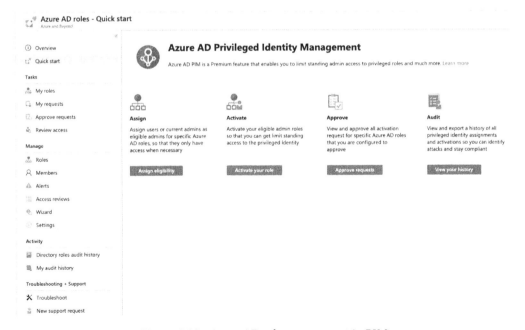

Figure. 3.33 - Azure AD role management in PIM

The **Manage** section offers all the Azure AD PIM configuration options for your Azure AD directory. **Roles** gives you an overview of all Azure AD roles and enables you to add members to a particular role. In the **Members** section, you get an overview about all accounts that are either eligible or permanent members of privileged roles. It is an at-a-glance view of all users that have elevated rights in your directory. The **Alerts** section shows you issues to review. For example, you will get an overview of administrators that are not using their privileged roles (and therefore can be unassigned). You can also create regular **Access reviews** to determine whether particular accounts still need to be role members. In the respective section, you find a configuration wizard to create these recurring reviews. The **Wizard** in the respective section leads you through a process to convert users with existing permanent role assignments into eligible users. Finally, in **Settings**, you can configure global settings for Azure AD roles, alerts, and access reviews.

> **Tip**
>
> You can require approval for a role activation. This requirement is a setting that comes with the role, not with the user account. That said, when you configure this requirement, it is valid for all users that are eligible to request access for this particular role.

Once an account is made eligible, its owner needs to request access before conducting a task. Let's walk through an example: John works in the helpdesk team and this team is responsible for managing user accounts. Therefore, we make John's account eligible for the *User Administrator* role. When John signs in to the Azure portal and then wants to manage user settings in Azure AD, he will only be able to see what usual user accounts are able to see; he won't be able to manage any accounts. So, John navigates to the Azure AD PIM dashboard and sees that he needs to activate his role first.

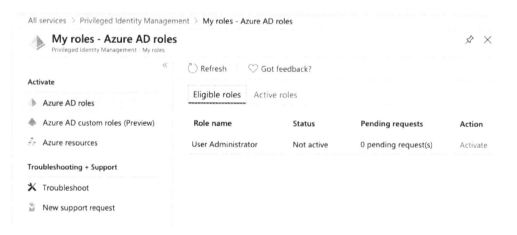

Figure. 3.34 - Eligible roles for a user

John can activate the role for the time that you configured before in the **Settings** pane for this particular role (all as the default for all roles). In the following example, the maximum activation duration is 1 hour only. In addition to that, we have enforced entering a justification that later can be reviewed in the audit history:

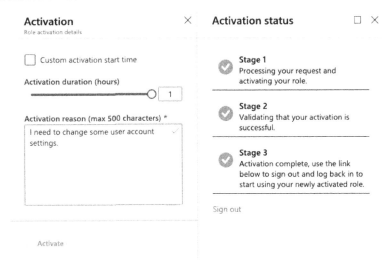

Figure. 3.35 - Activating a role

John could also set a custom activation start time. For example, when John knows that he will need access later that day, he could manually set an activation time in the future. With a click on **Activate,** an activation request is submitted and validated once the activation is done. Then, after signing out and logging back in, John will have role membership in User Administrators for 1 hour.

Figure. 3.36 - Successful role activation

So, the process for the user is straightforward. Request access; log out and back in again; and then do the job. Of course, every activation request is logged, as well as every configuration change a user does when having elevated rights. As already mentioned, monitoring is essential, and so there's no way around it.

Managing Azure resources with PIM

You can not only use PIM for managing Azure AD roles but also for Azure resource management based on RBAC. You first need to onboard Azure subscriptions to PIM so that you can use it to manage resource-based access rights. To do so, you navigate to **Azure resources** on the Azure AD PIM dashboard and select **Discover resources**. You then filter for unmanaged resources and select **Manage resource**, as illustrated in the following screenshot:

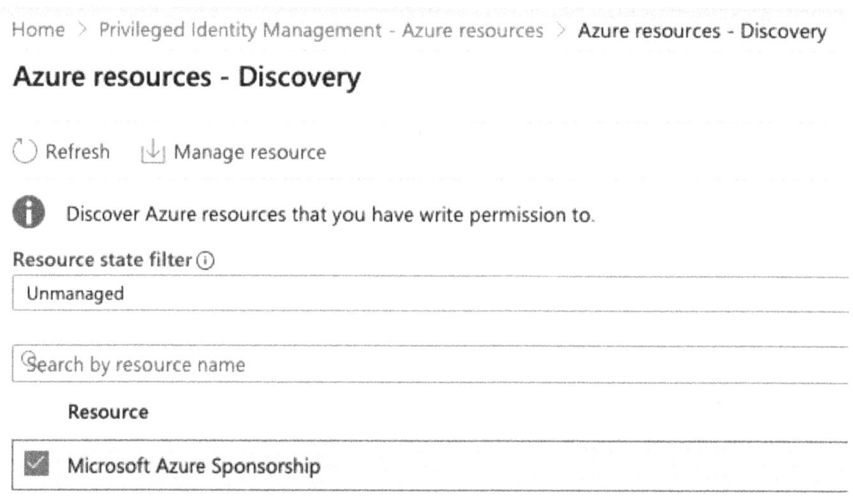

Home > Privileged Identity Management - Azure resources > **Azure resources - Discovery**

Azure resources - Discovery

◯ Refresh   ⬇ Manage resource

ⓘ Discover Azure resources that you have write permission to.

Resource state filter ⓘ

Unmanaged

Search by resource name

Resource

☑ Microsoft Azure Sponsorship

Figure. 3.37 - Onboarding an Azure subscription to PIM

You can also select a **Management** group to onboard to PIM. PIM will automatically manage role assignments for all child resources within the given scope after onboarding. The configuration options are similar to the ones for Azure AD management with PIM. One difference is that you need to enter a start and an end date for the role assignment. After the end date, the user will no longer be eligible for requesting access. The maximum is a time frame of 1 year.

Let's take an example. In his role as project owner for the Mastering Azure Security project, John needs to manage all resources within a particular resource group that has been created for this project. However, he should not be able to give other users or groups access to that resource group so access to the Contributor role should be the right one for him.

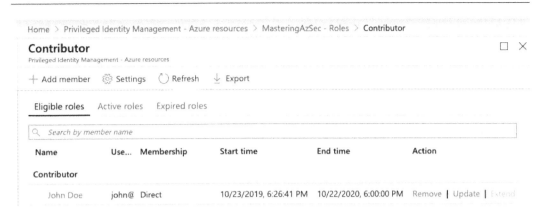

Figure. 3.38 - John is a member of the Contributor role via PIM

If John logs in to the Azure portal, he won't be able to see any resources or resource groups because he has no permanent access rights to Azure resources. Again, he navigates to the Azure AD PIM dashboard, selects Azure resources, and then activates his role. After logging out and signing in again, John is able to manage his resources in the **MasteringAzSec** resource group.

> **Tip**
> PIM always activates roles for 1 or several hours, even if access is only needed for 10 minutes. Therefore, users can find an option to deactivate roles after they have finished their tasks by navigating to **My roles** and then **Active roles** in both the **Azure AD roles** and the **Azure resources** sections.

You have now learned how to further reduce your privileged accounts' attack surfaces by using Azure AD PIM.

Hybrid authentication and SSO

Organizations have come a long way from an on-premises IT infrastructure since they started to roll out cloud-based **Software as a Service (SaaS)** applications such as Microsoft Office 365. Users usually do not want to keep track of several accounts and, as they already have a corporate account based on Windows Server AD, they usually want to also use that account for cloud-based authentications. Now, this is when Azure AD Connect comes into play.

Azure AD Connect is a directory replication service that helps you to synchronize existing user accounts from an on-premises Windows Server AD with Azure AD. This is a mandatory step because you can only grant access rights and licenses to cloud-based identities in Azure AD, not to on-premises accounts.

With Azure AD Connect, you have several options to provide a single sign-on experience to your users. In the following diagram, you can see a decision tree that helps you to decide which of them is the best for your organization:

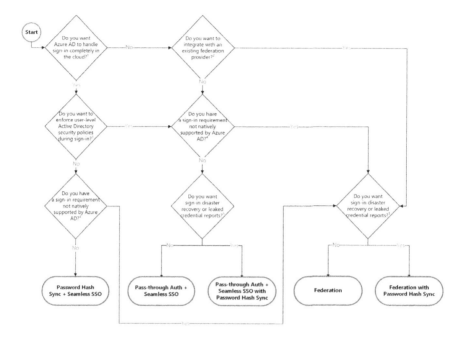

Figure. 3.39 - Azure AD Connect authentication decision tree

Password Hash Sync + Seamless SSO is the easiest way to go. With this, your on-premises password hashes are replicated to the corresponding cloud identities, so users can use the same usernames and passwords across all login environments. Seamless SSO eliminates unnecessary login prompts when users are signed in.

If you have stronger requirements, such as user-level AD security policies that should be enforced during sign-in, you can go with **Pass-through Auth + Seamless SSO**. In this scenario, you install a software agent on one or more on-premises servers. These servers can validate your user credentials directly against your on-premises domain controllers by building up a secure tunnel through which cloud-based logons can be validated.

Federation with **Active Directory Federation Services (AD FS)** or another federation service is the most complex authentication method. It should be used in scenarios where sign-in features are not natively supported by Azure AD. These features include the following:

- Sign-in using smartcards or certificates.
- Sign-in using an on-premises MFA server.

- Sign-in using a third-party authentication solution.
- Multi-site on-premises authentication solutions.

> **Tip**
> We recommend always enabling password hash synchronization in Azure
> AD Connect. Doing so, you have a fallback scenario in case your on-
> premises authentication platform is not working properly, and you can use
> Azure AD Identity Protection to get leaked credential reports. Furthermore,
> you can enable **self-service password reset (SSPR)** when password hash
> synchronization is enabled.

With SSPR, you can effectively reduce both users' non-effective time and support efforts
for your helpdesk team. SSPR provides users with an effective means to unblock their
corporate accounts if they forget their passwords. In order to use SSPR, users must
provide a secondary authentication method. When they lose access to their corporate
password, users need to verify their previously registered alternate authentication method
to prove their identity. After that, the user can enter a new password. If it is a hybrid user
account, meaning an account that is replicated by Azure AD Connect, the new password
is written back to the on-premises Active Directory. The feature you need to enable in
Azure AD Connect in this case is called *password writeback*.

Currently, there is a preview for the combined registration of SSPR and MFA that offers
you a new experience for your users' security registration.

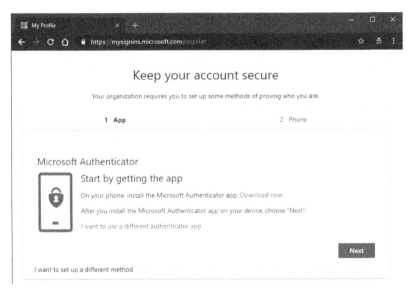

Figure. 3.40 - Combined registration for SSPR and MFA

Today, you can enable it for your Azure AD tenant by navigating to **Azure Active Directory** -> **User Settings** -> **Manage User Feature Preview Settings**. You can enable the preview features for all users or a selected group, as shown in the following screenshot:

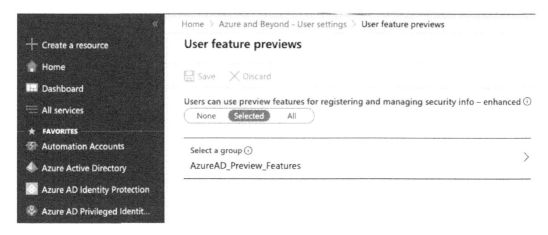

Figure. 3.41 - Enabling combined registration for SSPR and MFA in your tenant

After that, users for whom this setting applies are able to use the new experience at `https://myprofile.microsoft.com/`.

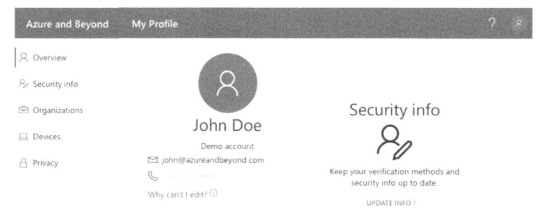

Figure. 3.42 - The new combined experience

Integrating on-premises identities into Azure AD is a great way to enhance the sign-in experience across your hybrid organization, and you just learned about the considerations to bear in mind before starting your hybrid journey. In the *Exploring passwords and passphrases* section, you learned that passwords are not good enough to protect your accounts. So, let's move on now to passwordless sign-ins in Azure AD.

Understanding passwordless authentication

In a world in which passwords are not enough to protect identities, we need another, more secure, approach to further protect identities. Passwords can be guessed or phished without physically having access to a user's device or storage. With passwordless authentication, Azure AD offers two different methods to sign in to a cloud-based user account without needing passwords anymore.

You can use the **Microsoft Authenticator app**, the app you already know from the *Understanding MFA* section. With this method, you are prompted to approve your sign-in by tapping a number in the Authenticator app, as shown in the following screenshot:

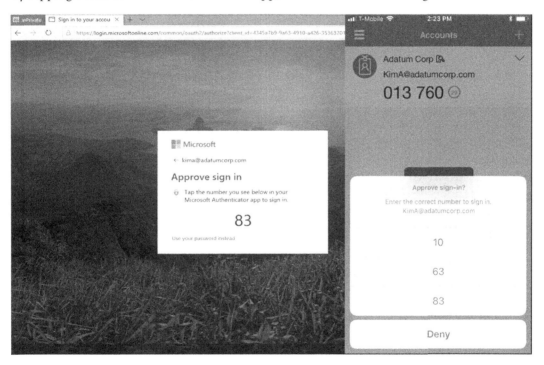

Figure. 3.43 - Phone-based passwordless authentication

All the user has to do is to register the app as an MFA option and then, in the smartphone app, choose **Enable phone sign-in** from the drop-down menu. After following the instructions in the app, the user can sign in to the app, without entering a password.

The second option is to use a **FIDO2 security key** to sign in against Azure AD. FIDO2-based passwordless authentication is currently in preview and is only supported on Windows 10 and in the Microsoft Edge browser.

Figure. 3.44 - FIDO2 security keys

Using this method, the user needs to have physical access to the security key that is needed during the authentication process. The user needs to be enabled for the enhanced security registration preview so access to the `https://myprofile.microsoft.com/` portal is enabled, as described in the *Hybrid authentication and SSO* section. To use a security key, it needs to be added to the user's security info, as shown in the following screenshot:

Security info

These are the methods you use to sign into your account or reset your password.

Default sign-in method: Microsoft Authenticator - notification Change

+ Add method

Phone		Delete

Add a method

Which method would you like to add?

Security key ⌄

Cancel   Add

Office phone   Delete

App password   Delete

Microsoft Authenticator   Delete

Figure. 3.45 - Associating a security key with a user's profile

After following the instructions, the user will be able to authenticate against Azure AD without entering a password.

Global settings

Before you can enable passwordless authentication on a per-user basis, the feature needs to be enabled for the Azure AD tenant. The settings can be found in the Azure AD portal under **Azure AD -> Security -> Authentication methods**, as shown in the following screenshot:

Figure. 3.46 - Enabling passwordless authentication for an Azure AD tenant

You have now learned how to enable passwordless authentication for your users. In the next section, you will learn about the licensing of security features in Azure AD.

Licensing considerations

Azure AD licensing can become a bit complex when it comes to security features. This is why we decided to compare different licenses and to explain which license you need for which feature. Azure AD is always licensed on a per-user basis, so you need one respective license for each user. For all security features that have been discussed in this chapter, you will either need an Azure AD Premium P1 or an Azure AD Premium P2 license. These licenses are also part of Microsoft 365 and **Enterprise Mobility + Security (EMS)** license packages.

- Microsoft 365 E3 contains EMS E3, which contains features of Azure AD Premium P1.

- Microsoft 365 E5 contains EMS E5, which contains features of Azure AD Premium P2.

- For the following features, you will need an Azure AD Premium P2 license:

- Azure AD PIM

- Azure AD Identity Protection

- Risk-based Conditional Access policies

For the following features, an Azure AD Premium P1 license is sufficient:

- Azure MFA

- Conditional Access based on group, location, and device status

- Self-service password reset

Summary

Identity is the new perimeter and so it's essential to properly protect user and administrator accounts in the cloud. In this chapter, you have learned why passwords are not enough to protect your accounts and how to protect them with MFA, Azure AD Identity Protection, and passwordless authentication. You are able to reduce your privileged accounts' attack surface as of now, to integrate Azure AD into your existing environments.

In the next chapter, you will learn how to protect network infrastructure resources on Azure and which platform services you need to achieve a better security posture.

Questions

1. With the cloud, identity is…

   A. More exposed to attacks

   B. Less exposed to attacks

   C. Equally exposed to attacks

2. We can control password settings with…

   A. Azure AD protection

   B. Account protection

   C. Password protection

3. We can increase account security with…

    A. More complex passwords

    B. More frequent password changes

    C. Multi-Factor Authentication (MFA)

    D. Two-Factor Authentication (2FA)

4. You can control actions that require MFA.

    A. Yes

    B. No

    C. Only for some actions

5. Which report is not available in risk detection?

    A. Users with leaked credentials

    B. Impossible travel

    C. Infected users

    D. Infected devices

6. With roles in **Privileged Identity Management (PIM)**, the user has…

    A. More privileges

    B. Fewer privileges

    C. To activate privileges

7. The most secure authentication is…

    A. A strong password

    B. MFA

    C. Passwordless

Section 2: Cloud Infrastructure Security

In this section, you will learn how to deploy infrastructure in a secure way and how to manage secrets and certificates in Microsoft Azure. You will also learn how to protect network resources and data in the cloud.

This section comprises the following chapters:

Chapter 4, Network Security

Chapter 5, Azure Key Vault

Chapter 6, Data Security

4
Azure Network Security

In *Chapter 1*, *Azure Security Introduction*, we briefly touched on network security in Azure, but only discussed how network security is handled by Microsoft inside Azure data centers. As the network also falls under the shared responsibility model, in this chapter, we will discuss network security from a user aspect and how to handle the security we are responsible for.

We will cover the following topics in this chapter:

- Understanding Azure Virtual Network
- Considering other virtual networks' security
- Understanding Azure Application Gateway
- Understanding Azure Front Door

Understanding Azure Virtual Network

The first step in the transition from an on-premises environment to the cloud is **Infrastructure as a Service (IaaS)**. One of the key elements in IaaS is **Virtual Networks (VNets)**. VNets are a virtual representation of our local network with IP address ranges, subnets, and all other network components that we would find in local infrastructure. Recently, we have seen a lot of cloud network components introduced to on-premises networks as well, with the introduction of **Software Defined Networking (SDN)** in OS Windows Server 2016.

Before we start looking at VNet security, let's remember that naming standards should be applied to all Azure resources, and networking is no exception. As environments grow, this will help you have better control over your environment, easier management, and more insight into your security posture.

Each VNet that we create is a completely isolated piece of network in Azure. We can create multiple VNets inside one subscription, or even multiple VNets inside one region. There is no direct communication between any VNets, even those created inside a single subscription or region, unless configured otherwise. The first thing that needs to be configured for a VNet is the IP address range. The next thing we need is a subnet with its own range. One VNet can have multiple subnets. Each subnet must have its own IP address range within the VNet's IP address range and cannot overlap with other subnets in the same VNet.

One thing we need to consider when defining the IP address range is that it should not overlap with other VNets we use. Even when there is no initial requirement to create a connection between different VNets, this may become a requirement in the future.

> **Important note**
> VNets that have overlapping IP ranges will not be compatible for connection.

VNets are used for communication between Azure resources over private IP addresses. Primarily, they're used for communication between Azure **Virtual Machines (VMs)**, but other resources can be configured to use private IP addresses for communication as well.

Communication between Azure VMs occurs over a **network interface card (NIC).** Each VM can be assigned one or more NICs, depending on the VM size. A bigger size allows more NICs to be associated with a VM. Each NIC can be assigned a private and public IP address. A private IP address is required and a public IP address is optional. As a NIC must have a private IP address, it must be associated with VNet and subnet on the same VNet.

As a first line of defense, we can use a **network security group (NSG)** to control traffic for Azure VMs. NSGs can be used to control inbound and outbound traffic. Default inbound and outbound rules are created during the NSG's creation, but we can change (or remove) these rules and create additional rules based on our requirements. The default inbound rules are shown in the following figure:

Priority	Name	Port	Protocol	Source	Destination	Action	
65000	AllowVnetinBound	Any	Any	VirtualNetwork	VirtualNetwork	⊘ Allow	⋯
65001	AllowAzureLoadBalancerinBound	Any	Any	AzureLoadBalancer	Any	⊘ Allow	⋯
65500	DenyAllInBound	Any	Any	Any	Any	⊘ Deny	⋯

Figure 4.1 – Inbound security rules

The default inbound rules will allow any traffic coming from within a VNet and any traffic forwarded from Azure Load Balancer. All other traffic will be blocked.

Conversely, the default outbound rule will allow almost any outbound traffic. The default rules will allow any outgoing traffic to a VNet or the internet, as in the following figure:

Priority	Name	Port	Protocol	Source	Destination	Action	
65000	AllowVnetOutBound	Any	Any	VirtualNetwork	VirtualNetwork	⊘ Allow	⋯
65001	AllowInternetOutBound	Any	Any	Any	internet	⊘ Allow	⋯
65500	DenyAllOutBound	Any	Any	Any	Any	⊘ Deny	⋯

Figure 4.2 – Outbound security rules

To add a new inbound rule, we need to define the source, source port range, destination, destination port range, protocol, action, priority, and name. Optionally, we can add a description that will help us understand why this rule was created. An example of how to create a rule to allow traffic over port 443 (HTTPS) is shown in the following figure:

Figure 4.3 – Adding new inbound security rules

Alternatively, we can create the same rule with Azure PowerShell:

1. First, we need to create a resource group where resources will be deployed:

```
New-AzResourceGroup -Name "Packt-Security" -Location `
"westeurope"
```

2. Next, we need to deploy VNet:

```
New-AzVirtualNetwork -Name "Packt-VNet"
-ResourceGroupName ` "Packt-Security" -Location
"westeurope" -AddressPrefix ` 10.11.0.0/16
```

3. And finally, we deploy NSG and create a rule:

New-AzNetworkSecurityGroup -Name "nsg1" -ResourceGroupName ` "Packt-Security" -Location "westeurope"

```
$nsg=Get-AzNetworkSecurityGroup -Name 'nsg1' `
-ResourceGroupName 'Packt-Security'
```

```
$nsg | Add-AzNetworkSecurityRuleConfig -Name 'Allow_
HTTPS' `
-Description 'Allow_HTTPS' -Access Allow -Protocol Tcp `
-Direction Inbound -Priority 100 -SourceAddressPrefix
Internet `
-SourcePortRange * -DestinationAddressPrefix * `
-DestinationPortRange 443 | Set-AzNetworkSecurityGroup
```

In order to add a new outbound rule, we need to define the same option as the inbound rule. An example of how to create a rule to deny traffic over port 22 is shown in the following figure:

Figure 4.4 – Adding new outbound security rules

Note that the priority plays a very important role when it comes to NSGs. A lower number means higher priority and a higher number means lower priority. If we have two rules that are in contradiction, the rule with the lower number will take precedence. For example, if we create a rule to allow traffic over port 443 with a priority of 100, and create a rule to deny traffic over port 443 with a priority of 400, traffic will be allowed, as the allow rule has a greater priority.

Again, we can use Azure PowerShell to create the rule:

```
$nsg | Add-AzNetworkSecurityRuleConfig -Name 'Allow_SSH' `
-Description 'Allow_SSH' `
-Access Allow -Protocol Tcp `
-Direction Outbound -Priority 100 `
-SourceAddressPrefix VirtualNetwork  -SourcePortRange * `
-DestinationAddressPrefix * -DestinationPortRange 22 `
| Set-AzNetworkSecurityGroup
```

An NSG can be associated with subnets and NICs. An NSG associated on a subnet level will have all the rules applied to all the devices associated with that subnet. When an NSG is associated with a NIC, rules will be applied only to that NIC. It's recommended to associate NSGs with subnets instead of NICs for more simple management. It's easy to manage traffic on a NIC level when we have fewer VMs. But when the number of VMs is in the dozens, hundreds, or even thousands, it becomes very hard to manage traffic on a NIC level. It's much better to have VMs that have similar requirements associated on a subnet level.

In order to associate an NSG with a subnet, follow these steps:

1. Go to the **Subnet** section under **NSG1** and select **Associate**, as in the following figure:

Figure 4.5 – NSG Subnets blade

2. Next, we select the virtual network, as in the following screenshot:

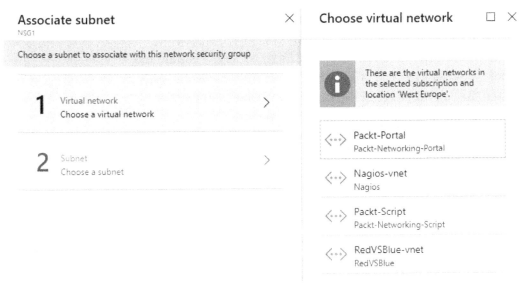

Figure 4.6 – VNet association to NSG

3. Finally, we select the subnet and confirm:

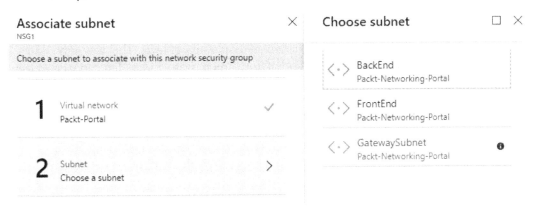

Figure 4.7 – Subnet association to NSG

Now all of the Azure VMs added to this subnet will have all the NSG rules applied immediately.

The Azure PowerShell script to associate an NSG with a subnet is the following:

```
$vnet = Get-AzVirtualNetwork -Name 'Packt-VNet' `
-ResourceGroupName 'Packt-Security'
Add-AzVirtualNetworkSubnetConfig -Name FrontEnd `
-AddressPrefix 10.11.0.0/24 -VirtualNetwork $vnet
$subnet = Get-AzVirtualNetworkSubnetConfig `
-VirtualNetwork $vnet -Name FrontEnd
$nsg = Get-AzNetworkSecurityGroup `
-ResourceGroupName 'Packt-Security' -Name 'nsg1'
$subnet.NetworkSecurityGroup = $nsg
Set-AzVirtualNetwork -VirtualNetwork $vnet
```

Let's take a simple three-tier application architecture as an example. Here, we would have VMs accessible from outside (over the internet), and these VMs should be placed in a DMZ subnet, which would be associated with an NSG that would allow such traffic. Next, we would have an application tier, which would allow traffic inside a VNet but no direct access over the internet.

The application tier would be associated with an appropriate subnet, which would (with the NSG on a subnet level) deny traffic over the internet but allow any traffic coming from the DMZ. Lastly, we would have a database tier, which would allow only traffic coming from the application tier, using the NSG associated on a subnet level. This way, any request would be able to reach the DMZ tier. Once a request is validated, it can pass to the application tier and from there it can reach the database tier. No direct communication is allowed between the DMZ and database tiers, and a direct request is not allowed to go from the internet to the application or database tiers.

For more security, resources can be associated with application groups. Using NSGs and application groups, we can create additional security rules with more network filtering options.

We will now be looking at connecting on-premises networks with Azure.

Connecting on-premises networks with Azure

In most cases, we already have some sort of local infrastructure and want to use the cloud as a hybrid where we combine cloud and on-premises resources. In such cases, we need to think about how we are going to access **Azure Virtual Network (VNet)** from our local network.

There are three options available:

- **Point-to-Site connection (P2S)** is usually used for management. It enables you to create a connection from a single on-premises computer to Azure VNet. It has a secure connection, but not the most reliable one, and shouldn't be used for production purposes, only to perform management and maintenance tasks.

- **Site-to-Site connection (S2S)** is a more stable connection that enables a network-to-network connection. In this case, that would be from an on-premises network to a VNet, where all on-premises devices can connect to Azure resources and vice versa. Using S2S enables you to expend local infrastructure to Azure, use hybrid cloud, and take advantage of the best things both on-premises and cloud networks can offer.

- **ExpressRoute** is a direct connection from a local data center to Azure. It doesn't go over the internet and offers a much better connection. Compared to an S2S connection, ExpressRoute offers more reliability and speed with lower network latency.

Next, we will be checking out how to create an S2S connection.

Creating an S2S connection

In order to create an S2S connection, several resources must be created. First, we need to create a **Virtual Network Gateway (VNG)**. During the process of creating a VNG, we need to define a subscription, a name for the VNG, the region where it will be created, and a VNet must be selected.

The VNet that we can select is limited to the region where the VNG will be created. A separate gateway subnet must be defined, so we can either select an existing one or it will be created automatically if it doesn't exist on the selected VNet.

In the same section, we need to define the public IP address (create a new one or select an existing one) and select to enable (or disable) active-active mode or BGP. An example is shown in the figure that follows.

The following details need to be filled in:

- **Subscription**
- **Instance details**
- **Public IP address**

You can see an example of this in the following figure:

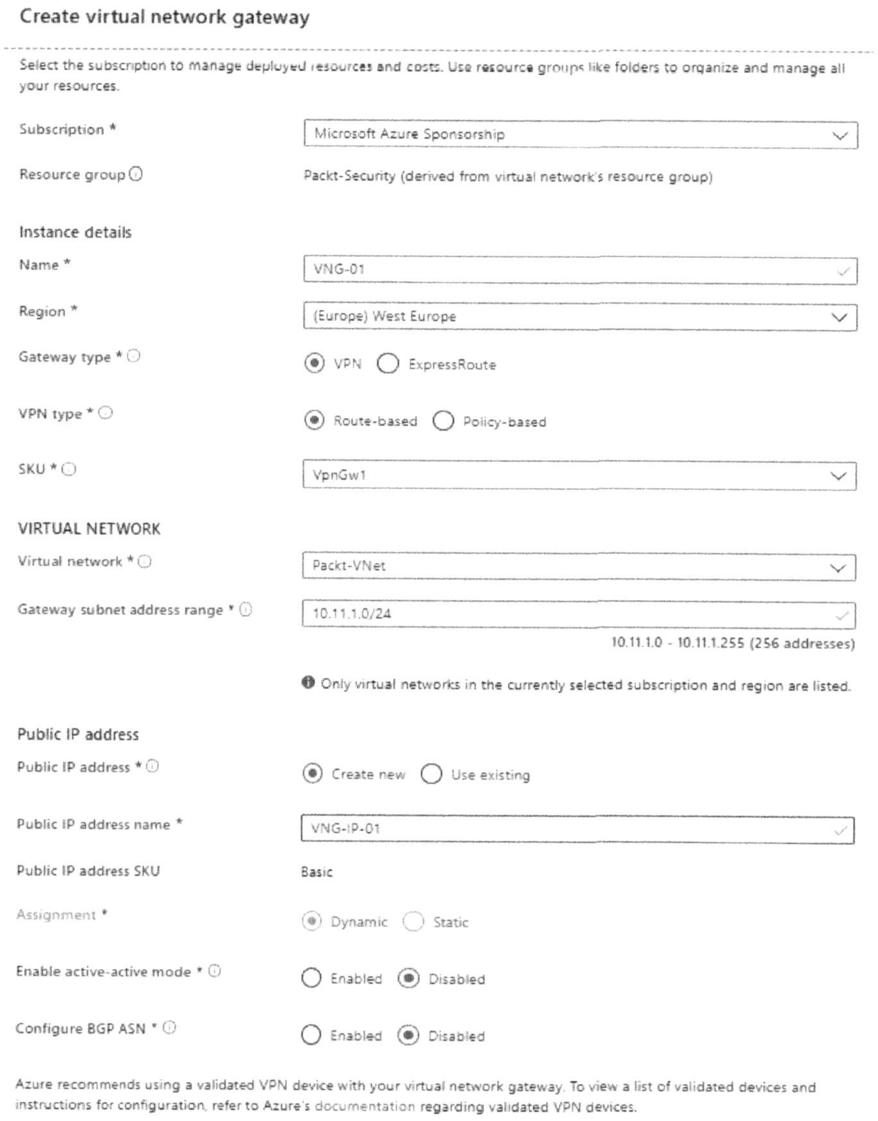

Create virtual network gateway

Select the subscription to manage deployed resources and costs. Use resource groups like folders to organize and manage all your resources.

Subscription *   Microsoft Azure Sponsorship

Resource group ⓘ   Packt-Security (derived from virtual network's resource group)

Instance details

Name *   VNG-01

Region *   (Europe) West Europe

Gateway type * ⓘ   ◉ VPN   ◯ ExpressRoute

VPN type * ⓘ   ◉ Route-based   ◯ Policy-based

SKU * ⓘ   VpnGw1

VIRTUAL NETWORK

Virtual network * ⓘ   Packt-VNet

Gateway subnet address range * ⓘ   10.11.1.0/24

                                  10.11.1.0 - 10.11.1.255 (256 addresses)

                                  ❶ Only virtual networks in the currently selected subscription and region are listed.

Public IP address

Public IP address * ⓘ   ◉ Create new   ◯ Use existing

Public IP address name *   VNG-IP-01

Public IP address SKU   Basic

Assignment *   ◉ Dynamic   ◯ Static

Enable active-active mode * ⓘ   ◯ Enabled   ◉ Disabled

Configure BGP ASN * ⓘ   ◯ Enabled   ◉ Disabled

Azure recommends using a validated VPN device with your virtual network gateway. To view a list of validated devices and instructions for configuration, refer to Azure's documentation regarding validated VPN devices.

Figure 4.8 – Creating a VNG

Another resource we need to create is a **Local Network Gateway (LNG)**. To create an LNG, we need to define the following:

- **Name**
- **IP address**

- **Address space**
- **Subscription**
- **Resource group**
- **Location**
- **BGP settings**

The BGP settings are optional. The IP address we need to define is the public IP address of our VPN device, and the address range is the address range of our local network. An example is shown in the following figure:

Figure 4.9 – Creating an LNG

After a VNG and an LNG are created, we need to create a connection in VNet:

1. Under the **connection settings** in the **VNet** blade, add a new connection.

2. The following parameters need to be defined: **Name**, **Connection type**, **Virtual network gateway**, **Local network gateway**, **Shared key (PSK)** and **IKE Protocol**.

3. **Subscription**, **Resource group** and **Location** will be locked and will use the same options as the ones assigned to the selected VNet:

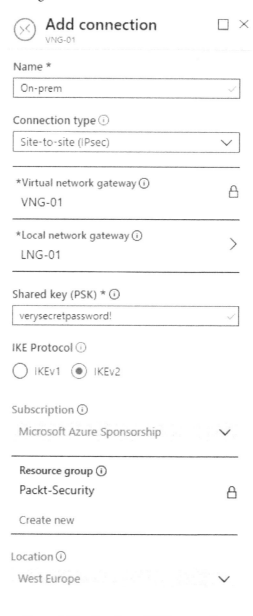

Figure 4.10 – Creating a VPN connection

After a connection is created in Azure, we still need to create a connection on our local VPN device. It's highly recommended to only use supported devices (most industry leaders are supported, such as Cisco, Palo Alto, and Juniper, to name a few). When configuring a connection on a local VPN device, we need to take into account all the parameters used on the Azure side.

Once a connection is configured on both sides, the tunnel is up and we should be able to access Azure resources from an on-premises network and from Azure to a local network. Of course, we can control how traffic flows and what can access what, how, and under which conditions.

We have now seen how to create connections between Azure VNets and local networks. But we often have a need to connect one VNet with another VNet. Of course, it's still important to keep the same level of security, even if everything is inside Azure. In the next section, we'll discuss how to connect networks in such a situation.

Connecting a VNet to another VNet

In a case where we have multiple VNets in Azure, we may need to create a connection between them in order to allow services to communicate between networks. There are two ways in which we can achieve this goal:

- The first one would be to create an S2S between the VNets. In this case, the process is very similar to creating an S2S between a VNet and a local network. We need to create a VNG for both VNets, but we don't need an LNG. When creating a connection, we need to select **VNet-to-VNet** in **Connection types** and select appropriate VNGs.

Another option would be to create VNet peering. An S2S connection is secure and encrypted, but it passes over the internet. Peering uses an Azure backbone network in order to route traffic, and it never leaves Azure. This makes peering even safer.

To create peering between VNets, we need to carry out the following steps:

1. Go to the peerings section in the VNet blade and add a new peering.

2. We need to define the name and the VNet we want to create a connection to.

3. Other settings are also present, such as whether we want to allow connections to go both ways, or whether we want to allow forwarded traffic.

A peering example is shown in the following figure:

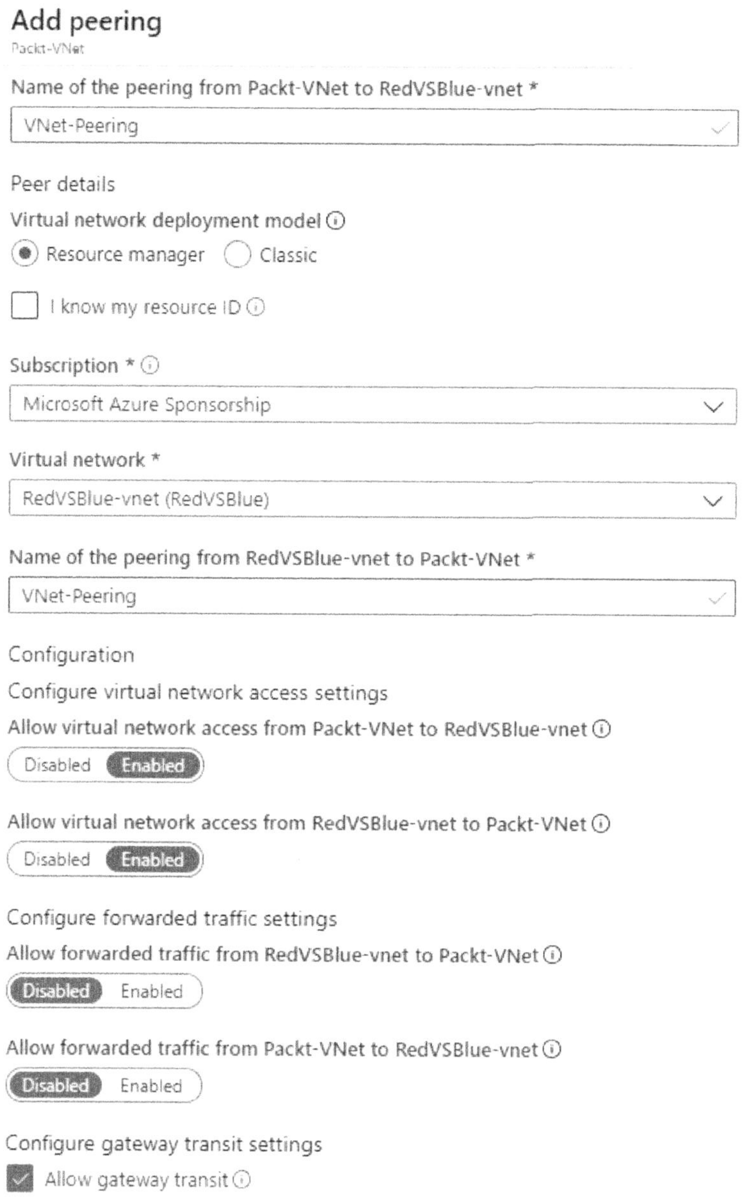

Add peering
Packt-VNet

Name of the peering from Packt-VNet to RedVSBlue-vnet *

    VNet-Peering

Peer details

Virtual network deployment model ⓘ

(•) Resource manager   ( ) Classic

[ ] I know my resource ID ⓘ

Subscription * ⓘ

    Microsoft Azure Sponsorship

Virtual network *

    RedVSBlue-vnet (RedVSBlue)

Name of the peering from RedVSBlue-vnet to Packt-VNet *

    VNet-Peering

Configuration

Configure virtual network access settings

Allow virtual network access from Packt-VNet to RedVSBlue-vnet ⓘ

(Disabled   **Enabled**)

Allow virtual network access from RedVSBlue-vnet to Packt-VNet ⓘ

(Disabled   **Enabled**)

Configure forwarded traffic settings

Allow forwarded traffic from RedVSBlue-vnet to Packt-VNet ⓘ

(**Disabled**   Enabled)

Allow forwarded traffic from Packt-VNet to RedVSBlue-vnet ⓘ

(**Disabled**   Enabled)

Configure gateway transit settings

[✓] Allow gateway transit ⓘ

Figure 4.11 – Creating VNet-to-VNet peering

It's very important to understand additional security settings in VNet peering and how they affect the network traffic.

The network access settings will define traffic access from one VNet to another. For example, we may want to enable access from **VNet A** to **VNet B**. But, because of security settings, we want to block access from **VNet B** to **VNet A**. This way, resources in **VNet A** will be able to access resources in **VNet B**, but resources in **VNet B** will not be able to access resources in **VNet A**:

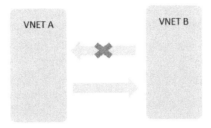

Figure 4.12 – VNet peering

In the next section, we will define how we handle forwarded traffic. Let's say that **VNet A** is connected to **VNet B** and **VNet C**. There is no connection between **VNet B** and **VNet C**. With these settings, we define whether we want to allow traffic from **VNet B** to reach **VNet C** over **VNet A**. The same thing can be defined the other way around:

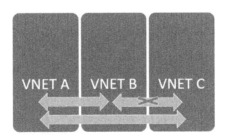

Figure 4.13 – VNet peering with multiple VNets

The gateway transit settings allow us to control whether we want a current connection to be able to use other connections with another network. For example, **VNet A** is connected to **VNet B** and **VNet B** is connected to an on-premises network (or another VNet). This setting will define whether traffic from **VNet A** will be able to reach the on-premises network. In this case, one of the VNets would be replaced with the on-premise network. If there is a connection between the on-premise network and **VNet A**, and a connection between **VNet A** and **VNet B**, the gateway transit would decide whether traffic from **VNet B** can reach the on-premise network.

In the next section, we will be discussing the most important thing when it comes to security, which is service endpoints in VNets.

VNet service endpoints

VNet service endpoints enable us to extend some **Platform as a Service (PaaS)** services to use private address spaces. With service endpoints, we connect services (that don't have this option by default) to our VNet enabling services to communicate over private IP addresses. This way, traffic is never exposed publicly, and data exchange is carried out over the Microsoft Azure backbone network.

Only some Azure services support this feature:

- Azure App Service
- Azure Container Registry
- Azure Cosmos DB
- Azure Data Lake
- Azure Database for MariaDB
- Azure Database for MySQL
- Azure Database for PostgreSQL
- Azure Event Hub
- Azure Key Vault
- Azure Service Bus
- Azure Storage
- Azure SQL Database
- Azure SQL Data Warehouse

The first security benefit from using service endpoints is definitely that data never leaves the private space. Let's say that we have Azure App Service and Azure SQL Database connected to the VNet with service endpoints. This way, all communication between the web application on App Service and the database on Azure SQL Database would be done securely over the VNet. No data would be exposed publicly, as is the case when using the same services without endpoints.

Without this feature, both services would only have public IP addresses and communication between them going over the internet. Even though there are ways of doing this securely, with communication being sent encrypted over HTTPS, using service endpoints partly removes the security risk in this communication.

But the security benefits of using service endpoints don't stop there. As services connected to VNet with service endpoints are assigned private IP addresses from a specific subnet, all security rules associated with this subnet are applied to our services as well. If an NSG blocks specific traffic on our subnet, the same traffic will be blocked for PaaS services as well.

We can enable service points on VNet either during the creation of a VNet or at a later time. Service endpoints are enabled on a subnet level, and this can be done either on a VNet or subnet configuration. Follow these steps to enable service endpoints in VNet:

1. Go to the VNet blade and select **service endpoints**. Click **add** and select the subnet and services you want to use, as in the following figure:

Figure 4.14 – Adding PaaS service endpoints

2. Go to the **subnet** configuration and select the services, as in the following figure:

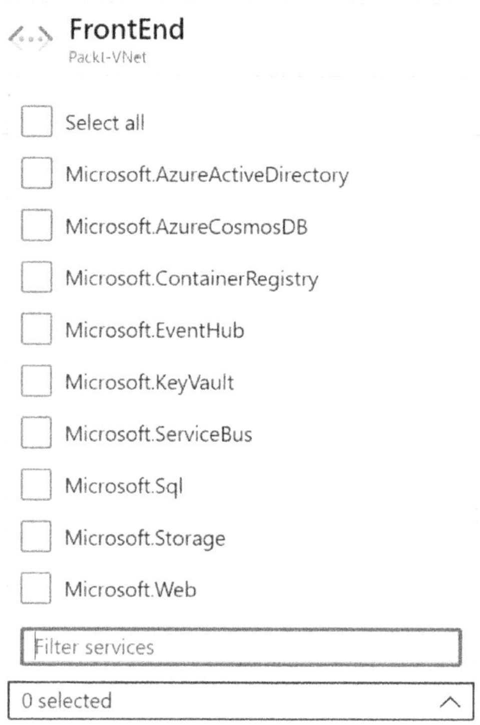

Figure 4.15 – Enabling service endpoints on subnet

Enabling service endpoints on a VNet and subnet is only half of the job. We need to enable settings on a PaaS service for the service endpoint to take effect. When enabling the service endpoint in the service settings, only subnets with enabled service endpoints will show up.

With service endpoints, we complete the network section that is available directly on Azure VNet settings. But there are other things we need to consider when it comes to network security. Let's see what else is available to increase network security in Azure.

Considering other virtual networks' security

For additional security and traffic control, a **Network Virtual Appliance (NVA)** can be used. An NVA can be deployed from Azure Marketplace. Once deployed, you will realize that an NVA, in fact, is an Azure VM with a third-party firewall installed. Most industry leaders are present in Azure Marketplace and we can deploy firewall solutions that we are used to in an on-premises environment. It's important to mention that we don't have to decide between NSGs or NVAs; these can be combined for additional security.

Additional network security can be achieved with Azure Firewall as well. Azure Firewall is a firewall as a service. It allows better network control than an NSG and can be compared to an NVA solution in many aspects. But Azure Firewall also has a few advantages compared to an NVA, such as built-in high availability, the option to deploy to multiple Availability Zones, and unrestricted cloud scalability. This means that no load balancers are needed. We can span Azure Firewall across multiple Availability Zones (and achieve an SLA of 99.99%), and scaling is configured to automatically accommodate any change in network traffic. Some options that are supported are: application filtering, network traffic filtering, FQDN tags, service tags, outbound SNAT support, inbound DNAT support, and multiple public IP addresses. With these options, we can have complete control of network traffic in our VNet. It's important to mention that Azure Firewall is compliant with many security standards, such as SOC 1 Type 2, SOC 2 Type 2, SOC 3, PCI DSS, and ISO 27001, 27018, 20000-1, 22301, 9001, and 27017.

Next, we will be looking at how to deploy and configure Azure Firewall through the Azure portal.

Azure Firewall deployment and configuration

This example – to deploy and configure Azure Firewall – requires Azure PowerShell. However, Azure Firewall can be configured and deployed through the Azure portal as well.

Azure Firewall deployment

In order to deploy Azure Firewall, we need to set up the required network and infrastructure:

1. First, we need to create subnets, create a VNet, and associate the subnets with the VNet:

```
$FWsub = New-AzVirtualNetworkSubnetConfig -Name `
AzureFirewallSubnet -AddressPrefix 10.0.1.0/26
$Worksub = New-AzVirtualNetworkSubnetConfig -Name
Workload-SN ` -AddressPrefix 10.0.2.0/24
$Jumpsub = New-AzVirtualNetworkSubnetConfig -Name Jump-SN
`
-AddressPrefix 10.0.3.0/24
$testVnet = New-AzVirtualNetwork -Name Packt-VNet `
-ResourceGroupName Packt-Security -Location "westeurope"
`
-AddressPrefix 10.0.0.0/16 -Subnet $FWsub, $Worksub,
$Jumpsub
```

2. Next, we need to deploy Azure VM, which will be used as a jump box (the VM we connect to in order to perform admin tasks on other VMs in the network; we don't connect to other VMs directly, but only through a jump box):

```
New-AzVm -ResourceGroupName Packt-Security -Name
"Srv-Jump" `
-Location "westeurope" -VirtualNetworkName Packt-VNet `
-SubnetName Jump-SN -OpenPorts 3389 -Size "Standard_DS2"
```

3. After the jump box, we create a test VM:

```
$NIC = New-AzNetworkInterface -Name Srv-work `
-ResourceGroupName Packt-Security -Location "westeurope"
`
-Subnetid $testVnet.Subnets[1].Id
$VirtualMachine = New-AzVMConfig -VMName Srv-Work -VMSize
` "Standard_DS2"
$VirtualMachine = Set-AzVMOperatingSystem -VM
$VirtualMachine `
-Windows -ComputerName Srv-Work -ProvisionVMAgent `
-EnableAutoUpdate
```

```
$VirtualMachine = Add-AzVMNetworkInterface -VM
$VirtualMachine ` -Id $NIC.Id
$VirtualMachine = Set-AzVMSourceImage -VM $VirtualMachine
`
-PublisherName 'MicrosoftWindowsServer' -Offer
'WindowsServer' ` -Skus '2016-Datacenter' -Version latest
New-AzVM -ResourceGroupName Packt-Security -Location `
"westeurope" -VM $VirtualMachine -Verbose
```

4. Finally, we deploy Azure Firewall:

```
$FWpip = New-AzPublicIpAddress -Name "fw-pip" `
-ResourceGroupName  Packt-Security -Location "westeurope"
`
-AllocationMethod Static -Sku Standard
$Azfw = New-AzFirewall -Name Test-FW01 -ResourceGroupName
`
Packt-Security -Location "westeurope" -VirtualNetworkName
` Packt-VNet -PublicIpName fw-pip
$AzfwPrivateIP = $Azfw.IpConfigurations.privateipaddress
```

5. Next, we will look at the Azure Firewall configuration.

The Azure Firewall configuration

After Azure Firewall is deployed, it doesn't actually do anything. We need to create a configuration and rules in order for Azure Firewall to be effective:

1. First, we will create a new route table with the BGP propagation disabled:

```
$routeTableDG = New-AzRouteTable -Name Firewall-rt-table `
-ResourceGroupName Packt-Security -location "westeurope" `
-DisableBgpRoutePropagation
Add-AzRouteConfig -Name "DG-Route" -RouteTable $routeTableDG `
-AddressPrefix 0.0.0.0/0 -NextHopType "VirtualAppliance" `
-NextHopIpAddress $AzfwPrivateIP | Set-AzRouteTable
Set-AzVirtualNetworkSubnetConfig -VirtualNetwork $testVnet `
-Name Workload-SN -AddressPrefix 10.0.2.0/24 `
-RouteTable $routeTableDG | Set-AzVirtualNetwork
```

2. Next, we create an application rule that allows outbound access to www.google.com:

```
$AppRule1 = New-AzFirewallApplicationRule -Name Allow-Google `
-SourceAddress 10.0.2.0/24 -Protocol http, https `
-TargetFqdn www.google.com
$AppRuleCollection =
New-AzFirewallApplicationRuleCollection `
-Name App-Coll01 -Priority 200 -ActionType Allow -Rule $AppRule1
$Azfw.ApplicationRuleCollections = $AppRuleCollection
Set-AzFirewall -AzureFirewall $Azfw
```

3. We then create a rule to allow a DNS on port 53:

```
$NetRule1 = New-AzFirewallNetworkRule -Name "Allow-DNS" `
-Protocol UDP -SourceAddress 10.0.2.0/24 `
-DestinationAddress 209.244.0.3,209.244.0.4
-DestinationPort 53
$NetRuleCollection = New-AzFirewallNetworkRuleCollection `
-Name RCNet01 -Priority 200 -Rule $NetRule1 -ActionType "Allow"
$Azfw.NetworkRuleCollections = $NetRuleCollection
Set-AzFirewall -AzureFirewall $Azfw
```

4. And then we need to assign a DNS to an NIC:

```
$NIC.DnsSettings.DnsServers.Add("209.244.0.3")
$NIC.DnsSettings.DnsServers.Add("209.244.0.4")
$NIC | Set-AzNetworkInterface
```

Try connecting to a jump box, and then through a jump box to test the VM. From the test VM, try resolving multiple URLs. Only www.google.com should succeed, as all outbound traffic is denied except for the explicit allow rule we created.

Let's move on to networking in PaaS and see what else is available, besides securing PaaS with service endpoints. We can have better network control and prevent unwanted traffic even with endpoints publicly available.

Understanding Azure Application Gateway

The next Azure service that can help increase security is Application Gateway. Application Gateway is a web-traffic load balancer that enables traffic management for web applications. It operates as **layer 7 (L-7, or application layer)** load balancing. This means that it supports URL-based routing and can route requests based on the URI path or host header.

Application Gateway supports **Secure Socket Layer (SSL/TSL)** termination at the gateway. After the gateway, traffic flows unencrypted to backend servers, which are unburdened from encryption and decryption overhead. However, if this is not an option because of security, compliance, or any other requirements, full end-to-end encryption is supported as well.

Application Gateway also supports scalability and zone redundancy. Scalability allows autoscaling depending on traffic load, and zone redundancy allows the service to be deployed to multiple availability zones in order to provide better fault resiliency, and removing the need to deploy the service to multiple zones manually.

Overall, Azure Application Gateway is an L-7 load balancer and we could question the security aspects of it (if we exclude SSL/TSL termination), as it's more a question of reliability and availability. But Application Gateway has an amazing security feature called Azure **Web Application Firewall (WAF)**. WAF protects web applications against common exploits and vulnerabilities.

WAF is based on the **Open Web Application Security Project (OWASP)** and is updated to address the latest vulnerabilities. As it's PaaS, all updates are done automatically without any user configuration. From a policy perspective, we can create multiple custom policies and apply different sets of policies to different web applications.

Two modes are available: detection and prevention. In detection mode, WAF will detect all suspicious requests but will not stop them, only log them. It's important to mention that WAF can be integrated with different logging tools, so logs can be stored for auditing purposes. When in protection mode, WAF will also block any malicious requests, return a `403 unauthorized access` exception, and close the connection. Prevention mode also logs all attacks.

Attacks are categorized by four severity levels:

- Critical (5)
- Error (4)
- Warning (3)
- Notice (2)

Each level has a severity value and the threshold for blocking is 5. So, a single critical issue is enough to block a session with value 5, but at least 2 error issues are needed to block a session, as 1 error with a value of 4 is below the threshold.

WAF works as a filter before Application Gateway – it will process a request, decide whether it's valid or not, and, based on this decision, it will allow the request to proceed to Application Gateway or reject the request. Once the request is allowed by WAF, Application Gateway acts as a normal L-7 load balancer, as if WAF was turned off. You can see that in the following figure:

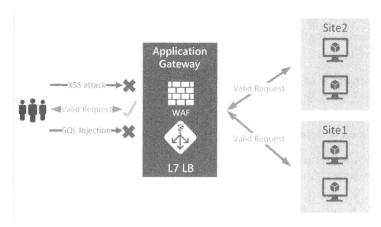

Figure 4.16 – Application Gateway traffic flow

Some of the attacks that can be detected and prevented with WAF are listed here:

- SQL injection
- Cross-site scripting
- Command injection
- Request smuggling
- Response splitting
- HTTP protocol violations and anomalies
- Protection against crawlers and scanners
- Geo-filter traffic

WAF on Application Gateway supports logging options to Azure Monitor, diagnostic logs to storage accounts, and integration with security tools such as Azure Security Center or Azure Sentinel.

Understanding Azure Front Door

Azure Front Door works very similarly to Application Gateway but on a different level. Like Application Gateway, it's an L-7 load balancer with an SSL offload. The difference is that Application Gateway works with services in a single region where Azure Front Door allows us to define, manage, and monitor routing on a global level. With Azure Front Door, we can ensure the highest availability using global distribution. A similar thing can be achieved with Azure Traffic Manager (in terms of global distribution), but this service lacks L-7 load balancing and SSL offloading.

What Azure Front Door provides actually combines Application Gateway and Traffic Manager to enable an L-7 load balancer with global distribution. It's also important to mention that a WAF is also available on Azure Front Door. Using a WAF on Azure Front Door, we can provide web application protection for globally distributed applications.

Summary

In this chapter, we addressed network security and, prior to that, we saw how to manage cloud identities. We need to remember that network security doesn't stop with IaaS and VNets. Network security basics are usually associated with VNets and NSGs. But even with IaaS, it does not stop there, and we have options to extend with an NVA or Azure Firewall. With PaaS, we can leverage VNet's service endpoints but extend security with services like Application Gateway or Azure Front Door.

But, with all the preclusions limiting who, how, when, and from where we can access our resources, we still need to handle sensitive information and data. The next chapter will address how can we manage certificates, secrets, passwords, and connection strings using Azure Key Vault.

Questions

1. We can control traffic in virtual networks with…

   A. A network interface

   B. A Network Security Group (NSG)

   C. An Access Control List (ACL)

2. What type of connection is available with on-premises networks?

   A. Point-to-Site

   B. Site-to-Site

   C. VNet-to-VNet

3. A connection between Virtual Networks can be made with…

    A. VNet-to-VNet

    B. VNet peering

    C. Both of the above

    D. None of the above

4. Which feature allows us to connect PaaS services to a virtual network?

    A. Service connection

    B. Service endpoints

    C. ExpressRoute

5. When multiple networks are involved…

    A. We can define a route

    B. Traffic is blocked by default

    C. Traffic is allowed by default

    D. A and B are correct

    E. A and C are correct

6. Which feature in Application Gateway adds additional security?

    A. Open Web Application Security Project (OWASP)

    B. Web Application Firewall (WAF)

    C. Secure Socket Layer (SSL) / Transport Layer Security (TSL)

7. What type of attack cannot be blocked with Application Gateway?

    A. SQL injection (SQLi)

    B. Cross-Site Scripting (XSS)

    C. Distributed Denial of Service (DDoS)

    D. HTTP protocol violations

5
Azure Key Vault

When talking about cloud computing, discussions are often directed towards data protection, encryption, compliance, data loss (and data loss prevention), trust, and other buzzwords that center around the same group of topics. What they all have in common is the need for a trusted service that helps them to secure cloud data without giving a cloud vendor access to both your data and the corresponding encryption keys. Let's imagine that you want to create an Azure resource, like a virtual machine, that you will need admin credentials for. In this case, you don't want to hard code usernames and passwords in your deployment script or template, do you? This is a scenario where Azure Key Vault comes into play. In this chapter, we will cover the following topics:

- Understanding Azure Key Vault
- Understanding service-to-service authentication
- Using Azure Key Vault in deployment scenarios

Understanding Azure Key Vault

Azure Key Vault is a secure, cloud-based storage solution for keys, secrets, and certificates. Tokens, passwords, certificates, API keys, and other secrets can be securely stored and access to them can be granularly controlled using Azure Key Vault. The service can also be used as a key-management solution. Azure Key Vault makes it easy to create and control the encryption keys that are used to encrypt your data. Another usage scenario is Secure Sockets Layer/Transport Layer Security (SSL/TLS) certificate enrolment and management. You can use Azure Key Vault to address certificate lifecycle management for both Azure and internally connected resources. Secrets and keys that are stored in an Azure Key Vault can be protected either by software or HSMs (hardware security modules) that are FIPS 140-2 Level 2 validated.

As you have already learned, you can use Azure Key Vault to manage keys, secrets, and certificates.

- A cryptographic key is used for data encryption. Azure Key Vault represents keys as **JSON Web Key** (**JWK**) objects, which are declared as soft or hard keys. A hard key is processed in a **hardware security module** (**HSM**), whereas a soft key is processed in the software by Azure Key Vault. A soft key is still encrypted at rest using a hard key, which is stored in an HSM. Clients can either request Azure Key Vault to generate a key or import an existing RSA or **elliptic curve** (**EC**) key. RSA and EC are the algorithms that are supported by Azure Key Vault.

- A secret is basically a string that is encrypted and stored in Azure Key Vault. A secret can be used to securely store passwords, storage account keys, and other highly valuable strings.

- A certificate in Azure Key Vault is an x509 certificate that is issued by a **public key infrastructure** (**PKI**). You can either let Azure Key Vault request a certificate from a supported public **certification authority** (**CA**), which today are DigiCert and GlobalSign, or you can create a **certificate signing request** (**CSR**) within Azure Key Vault and manually let this CSR be signed by any public CA of your choice.

In this chapter, you will learn how to work with key vault entities. But first, let's look at service-to-service authentication in Azure Key Vault, which is needed to enable other Azure services to leverage Azure Key Vault during deployment or resource-management operations.

Access to an Azure key vault is granted by RBAC. That said, you need to have an Azure AD account to get access to the service, which means that you can use all the protective options for interactive authentications that were discussed in *Chapter 3, Managing Cloud Identities*. Furthermore, access to items protected by Azure key vault can be restricted to only single aspects of Azure Key Vault. For example, an account could be granted access only to secrets, but not to keys or certificates, or you could grant an account only a subset of permissions, but for all entities stored in a key vault. This granular rights management, in addition to RBAC, which will only grant access to an Azure key vault (being an Azure resource), is implemented by access policies. Let's look at these policies in a little more detail in the next section.

Understanding access policies

With access policies, you can granularly define who will get what level of access rights to a single Azure Key Vault instance:

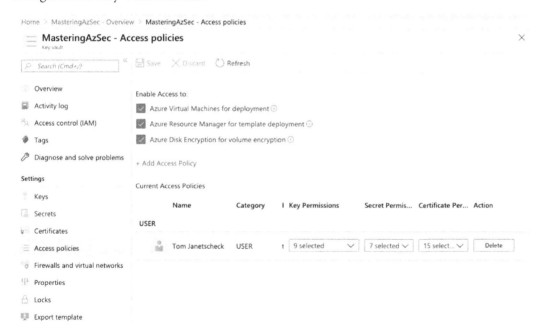

Fig. 5.1 – Azure Key Vault access policies

As you can see in the preceding screenshot, the user account called Tom has been granted several permissions to access keys, secrets, and certificates in the **Access policies** settings section of the Azure Key Vault **MasteringAzSec** section. Besides that, you can enable access to keys and secrets for Azure VMs, ARM, and Azure Disk Encryption. These options are necessary if you want to grant Azure VMs in your tenant read access to secrets so that they can be retrieved during VM deployments or if you want to enable Azure Resource Manager to retrieve secrets so they can be used in a template deployment. The third option specifies whether Azure Disk Encryption—a service that encrypts Azure VMs' disks using BitLocker or dm-crypt, depending on the operating system used in the Azure VM—is allowed to retrieve secrets from the Azure key vault and unwrap values from stored keys.

Before we move on to learn more about service-to-service authentication with Azure Key Vault, let's first take a deeper look at what the single entities in Azure Key Vault are.

Understanding service-to-service authentication

As we mentioned before, access to an Azure key vault and its entities is usually granted on a per-user basis. That said, to enable service-to-service authentication, you could create an Azure AD application with associated credentials and use this service principal to get an access token for your application. It's a pretty straightforward process:

1. Go to **Azure Active Directory | App registrations** in the Azure portal and select **New registration** to start the wizard:

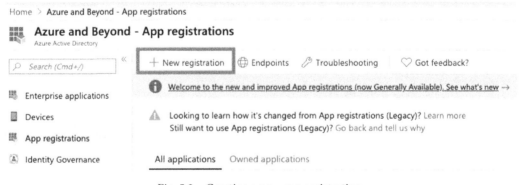

Fig. 5.2 – Creating a new app registration

2.   Enter a name and confirm your choice.

3.   Create a client secret by navigating to the **Certificates & secrets** option in the app registration and then select **New client secret**:

Fig. 5.3 – Creating a new client secret

4.   Enter a description and decide whether the secret will expire in 1 or 2 years, or whether it will always be valid. After confirming your choices and leaving the wizard, you are presented with the new client secret and its value, which you can copy and then use for authentication:

Client secrets

A secret string that the application uses to prove its identity when requesting a token. Also can be referred to as application password.

+ New client secret		
Description	Expires	Value
my client secret	11/14/2020	hzBS5v28/SW5SirPBEFQsVKq:.nEdBu:

Fig. 5.4 – Your client secret

A quicker way is to use the Azure CLI. With the following command, you can simply create a new service principal with the name MasteringAzSecSP:

```
Az ad sp create-for-rbac --name MasteringAzSecSP
```

The engine will use default settings for the account creation, and once the process is finished, you will find the username `appId` and the client secret password in the CLI window, as shown in the following screenshot:

```
[MacBookPro:~ tom$ az ad sp create-for-rbac --name MasteringAzSecSP
Changing "MasteringAzSecSP" to a valid URI of "http://MasteringAzSecSP", which i
s the required format for service principal names
Creating a role assignment under the scope of "/subscriptions/

  Retrying role assignment creation: 1/36
{
  "appId": "2ac48c3b-db12-4365-b59f-b86d4653a37a",
  "displayName": "MasteringAzSecSP",
  "name": "http://MasteringAzSecSP",
  "password": "883d4d62-f65c-4426-8731-42c208116ad5",
  "tenant": '
}
MacBookPro:~ tom$
```

Fig. 5.5 – Using the Azure CLI to create a new service principal

The service principal behaves similarly to a user account in terms of access management, which means that you can use the username (the application or client ID) as a principal when granting access to the key vault and its entities.

While this approach works great, there are two downsides that come with it:

- When creating the application credentials, you will get the app ID and the client secret, which are usually hardcoded in your source code. It's a dilemma, because you cannot store these credentials in Azure Key Vault as they are needed to authenticate before being granted access to the key vault.

- Application credentials expire and the renewal process may cause application downtime. You don't want to use a client secret that will never expire and that is hardcoded in your source code.

So, for automated deployments, we need another approach, which is where the **Managed Identities for Azure Resources** service comes into play. So let's move one step further and learn how this service can address the dilemma.

Understanding Managed Identities for Azure Resources

Needing credentials to get access to services is a common problem that you will often encounter. Azure Key Vault is an important part of your application design because you can use it to securely store and manage credentials for other services. But Azure Key Vault itself is a service that requires authentication before you are granted access. With *Managed Identities for Azure Resources*, a free feature of Azure Active Directory, you can solve this dilemma. The service provides other Azure services with an automatically managed identity in Azure AD.

There are two different types of managed identities within the service:

- A system-assigned managed identity is directly enabled on an instance of an Azure service. When the managed identity is enabled, Azure AD automatically creates an identity for the particular service in Azure AD that is automatically trusted by the Azure subscription that the service instance is created in. The credentials are automatically provided to the service instance after the identity is created. The identity's lifecycle is directly tied to the service's lifecycle, which means that a system-assigned managed identity is automatically removed from Azure AD when the service is deleted.

- A user-assigned managed identity is a manually created Azure resource. When creating a user-assigned managed identity, Azure AD will create a service principal in the Azure AD tenant that is trusted by the Azure subscription you are currently using. After creating the identity, you can assign it in one or several Azure service instances. The user-assigned managed identity's lifecycle is organized separately from the services' lifecycles that the identity is assigned to. In other words, when an Azure resource with a user-assigned managed identity is deleted, the managed identity is not automatically removed from Azure AD.

The relationship between a system-assigned managed identity and an Azure resource is 1:1, which means that an Azure resource can only have one system-assigned managed identity and this identity is only usable by the particular service it was created for.

The relationship between the user-assigned managed identity and the Azure resource is n:n, which means that you can use several user-assigned managed identities with one Azure resource at the same time, and that a single user-assigned managed identity can be used by several different Azure resources.

> **Important Note**
> Microsoft provides a list of Azure services that currently support system-assigned, user-assigned, or both types of managed identities at `https://docs.microsoft.com/en-us/azure/active-directory/managed-identities-azure-resources/services-support-managed-identities`.

The creation process of a system-assigned managed identity in the Azure portal is very easy. All Azure resources that currently support managed identities have an **Identity** option in the resource's **Settings** section:

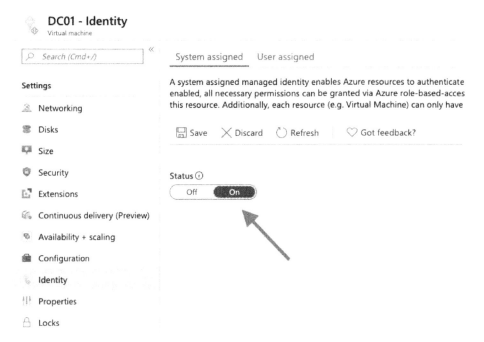

Fig. 5.6 – Activating a system-assigned managed identity for an Azure virtual machine

The following steps show you how to activate a system-assigned managed identity for an Azure virtual machine:

1. On the **Settings** page, you can choose whether you want to activate a system-assigned managed identity or whether you want to assign a user-assigned managed identity. To activate a system-assigned managed identity, you just have to set the **Status** toggle switch to **On** and then save your selection, as shown in the preceding screenshot.

2. You will then be informed that once you confirm this configuration, a managed identity for your resource will be registered in Azure AD, and that once the process has finished, you can grant permissions to that particular managed ID. In the preceding example, I have enabled a system-assigned managed identity for an Azure VM with the name DC01.

3. When creating a new key vault access policy, we can now select the identity with the same name to grant access to the key vault's entities.

If you want to create a new user-assigned managed identity, you have to navigate to the managed identity service in the Azure portal:

1. To do so, go to **All resources** and then search for **Managed Identities**.

2. Once you find the dialog, you can choose to create a new user-assigned managed identity. As mentioned before, this is a new Azure resource and therefore needs to be created in an Azure subscription and stored in an Azure resource group:

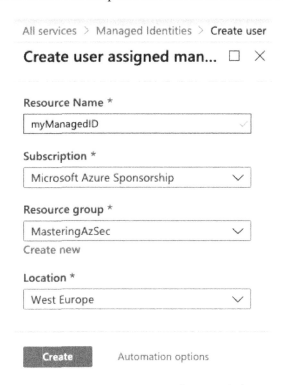

Fig. 5.7 – Creating a user-assigned managed identity

3.   Once the user-assigned managed identity is created, you can assign it to your Azure resource, like the virtual machine we used in the preceding scenario.

Managed identities can also be used for Azure DevOps or Terraform authentication against your Azure environment.

> **Important Note**
>
> You can also use the Azure CLI, PowerShell, ARM templates, and Terraform to create managed identities in Azure. You can find examples of these methods in the GitHub repository that has been created for this book, at `https://github.com/PacktPublishing/Mastering-Azure-Security`.

Let's assume that you only want to allow Azure resource creation via a DevOps pipeline with all related processes, such as pull requests, authoring, and so on. From a technical point of view, Azure DevOps is nothing but an application that needs to be granted access to an Azure subscription (or management group). Therefore, Azure DevOps needs a service principal that is either manually managed as an application registration with all its downsides, or that can be automatically managed using a managed identity. The same applies to Terraform, which is also just an application that needs rights in an Azure environment.

> **Important Note**
>
> You can use a managed identity for Terraform authentication against Azure AD; however, in this case, the managed identity is created for an Azure VM and Terraform needs to be started from within the VM so that it can make use of the ID.

Now that you know how managed identities work and what options you have for service-to-service authentication, let's move one step forward and see how you can use Azure Key Vaults in your deployment scenarios.

Using Azure Key Vault in deployment scenarios

Azure Key Vault is a nice service when it comes to securely storing and retrieving credentials that are needed during resource creation. It also helps you to encrypt Azure resources, such as Azure storage accounts or VM disks, with your own encryption key.

In this section, we will cover several options for how to use Azure Key Vault in deployment scenarios. You will find examples for PowerShell, ARM templates, and Terraform, as these are the most common deployment tools when it comes to creating Azure resources.

> **Important Note**
>
> The first step you will always have to go through is to authenticate with Azure AD using a principal that has been assigned the appropriate set of access rights in the Azure environment that you want to deploy resources to, depending on the task you want to perform and the resource that is affected by it.

Are you ready? Then let's start by creating a new Azure key vault and a secret that can later be used in a VM deployment scenario in the following section.

Creating an Azure key vault and a secret

As with all Azure resources, you can use the Azure portal to create and manage an Azure key vault. Although it might be convenient to click through the portal, it is a better idea to use a scripting or template language for this. Azure Key Vault is a critical resource when it comes to automated deployments. Today, there is no way to granularly grant access to single items of the same type within the same key vault. You can manage levels of access to keys, secrets, and certificates, but only on a key-vault level, not on an item level. This is why you might want to create several key vaults in the same Azure subscription. Using deployment automation, you can make sure that all key vaults in your environment adhere to the rules and policies you have defined.

Key vault creation in PowerShell

With PowerShell being an imperative scripting language, you need to define all the steps that are necessary in the correct order:

1. The first thing you need to do is to log in with an account that has the appropriate set of access rights to create a new resource group and Azure key vault instance in your Azure subscription:

```
# Login to your Azure subscription
Login-AzAccount
```

2. You will then be prompted to enter your Azure login credentials, which are used by PowerShell to go through the next steps. After logging in, you either create a new resource group or refer to an existing one.

3. We will now assume that a new RG will be created using the following code snippet. Before we do so, it makes sense to define all values for variables that are then used in the following script sections:

```
# Define variable values
$rgName = "myResourceGroup"
$azRegion= "WestEurope"
$kvName = "myAzKeyVault"
$secretName = "localAdmin"
$localAdminUsername = "myLocalAdmin"
# Create a new resource group in your Azure suscription
$resourceGroup = New-AzResourceGroup `
-Name $rgName `
-Location $azRegion
```

4. Now you can move on and create a new Azure key vault:

```
# Create a new Azure Key Vault
New-AzKeyVault `
     -VaultName $kvName `
     -ResourceGroupName $rgName `
     -Location $azRegion `
     -EnabledForDeployment `
     -EnabledForTemplateDeployment `
     -EnabledForDiskEncryption `
     -Sku standard
```

In the preceding script, there are some mandatory and optional parameters listed. It is mandatory to use the following parameters when creating a new Azure key vault:

- VaultName defines the name of the Azure key vault. We are using the $kvName variable, which is defined at the beginning of the script.

- ResourceGroupName defines the Azure resource group that the key vault will be created in.

- Location defines the Azure region that the key vault will be created in.

There are also some optional parameters that are defined in the preceding section:

- `EnabledForDeployment` enables the `Microsoft.Compute` resource provider to retrieve secrets from the Azure key vault during resource creation—for example, when deploying a new VM.

- `EnabledForTemplateDeployment` enables the **Azure Resource Manager (ARM)** to get secrets for an Azure key vault when it is referenced in a template deployment, such as when you are using ARM or Terraform.

- `EnabledForDiskEncryption` enables the **Azure Disk Encryption** service to get secrets and unwrap keys from an Azure key vault to use them in the disk encryption process.

- `SKU` defines the Azure key vault's SKU (standard or premium).

5. After the Azure key vault has been created, you need to create an access policy. In the following example, we grant access rights to secrets in the new Azure key vault for the currently logged-in user account:

```
# Grant your user account access rights to Azure Key
Vault secrets
Set-AzKeyVaultAccessPolicy `
    -VaultName $kvName `
    -ResourceGroupName $rgName `
    -UserPrincipalName (Get-AzContext).account.id `
    -PermissionsToSecrets get, set
```

6. You can then create a new key vault secret. In the following snippet, you enter the secret as a secure string in the PowerShell session:

```
# Create a new Azure Key Vault secret
$password = read-host -assecurestring
Set-AzKeyVaultSecret `
    -VaultName $kvName `
    -Name $secretName `
    -SecretValue $password
```

Congratulations! You have just created your first Azure key vault and a secret using PowerShell. Now, that you know how to create an Azure key vault and a key vault secret for your deployment scenario, we can move on to the next section, *Azure VM deployment*, in which you will learn how to use the resources that you have just created in a more complex scenario.

Azure VM deployment

When deploying an Azure VM, you always need to pass local admin credentials to it during the deployment process. The downside of deploying VMs using the Azure portal is that you need to manually enter the respective local admin credentials instead of using a secret that is stored in an Azure key vault. This is only one of the reasons why infrastructure-as-code deployments definitely make sense in an enterprise environment. In this section, you will learn how to reference credentials that are stored in an Azure key vault instead of hardcoding the information in the deployment script or template.

We will start by referencing a key vault secret for VM deployments using PowerShell.

VM deployments with PowerShell

You can easily access secrets in an Azure key vault with PowerShell, but also with ARM templates and Terraform. Let's see how we can do this by going through the following steps:

1. After you have retrieved a secret, you need to create a new `PSCredential` object that can be used in the VM deployment, as follows:

    ```
    # retrieve an Azure Key Vault secret
    $secret = Get-AzKeyVaultSecret `
        -VaultName $kvName `
        -Name $secretName
    # Create a new PSCredential object
    $cred = [PSCredential]::new($localAdminUsername,$secret.
    SecretValue)
    ```

2. Later, you can use this `PSCredential` object in your deployment in the respective position. This would look similar to the following code snippet:

    ```
    $myVM = Set-AzVMOperatingSystem `
        -VM $myVM `
        -Windows `
        -ComputerName $vmName `
        -Credential $cred `
        [...]
    ```

It is always a good idea to work with variables in a PowerShell script. By doing so, you can have a variable section at the beginning of the script where you can define values that change depending on your needs and the environments that the script is used in.

> **Tip**
>
> Since the complete VM deployment script in PowerShell consists of almost 200 lines, we have not printed it in the book, but have published it in the book's GitHub repository.

PowerShell is a good way to deploy Azure resources, but being an imperative scripting language, it is not the best fit for usage in DevOps/CI/CD scenarios. This is why we will explain how to reference a key vault secret in Terraform in the next section.

Referencing a key vault secret in Terraform

In Terraform, you can refer to an existing Azure object with data sources. For a key vault secret, the data source is called `azurerm_key_vault_secret`:

```
# Azure Key Vault data source to access local admin password
data "azurerm_key_vault_secret" "mySecret" {
    name = "secretName"
    key_vault_id = "/subscriptions/GUID/resourceGroups/RGName/providers/Microsoft.KeyVault/vaults/VaultName"
}
```

This object can then be referenced in the `os_profile` section of a Terraform deployment template, as shown in the following screenshot:

```
os_profile {
    computer_name = "myVM"
    admin_username = "myLocalAdminUserName"
    admin_password = "$(data.azurerm_key_vault_secret.mySecret.value)"
}
```

Terraform is quite an easy way of deploying and referencing Azure resources. As you can see from the preceding examples, you simply need to define a data source and then reference it in the respective resource section of your deployment template.

> **Tip**
>
> We have published a complete example for a VM deployment with Terraform in this book's GitHub repository:
> `https://github.com/PacktPublishing/Mastering-Azure-Security`

ARM templates are Microsoft's way of using automatic Azure resource deployments in DevOps pipelines. This example is described in detail in the following section.

Referencing a key vault secret in ARM templates

ARM templates might be the most complex way to refer to key vault secrets during a template deployment. This is because you need to use linked templates in this scenario. That said, you need to have two different template files that are used for different purposes.

The main template is used as a reference to existing Azure resources, such as the Azure key vault and its secrets. In it, there is a `parameters` section that contains values that are either defined directly in the main template or passed to the template by an external call that is an Azure CLI or a PowerShell call and then passed directly to the linked template.

If the `parameters` section is filled by pipeline input, it will only contain the parameters' definitions:

```
"parameters": {
    "vaultName": {
     "type": "string"
    },
    "vaultResourceGroup": {
     "type": "string"
    },
    "secretName": {
     "type": "string"
    }
}
```

If the parameters' values are defined within the main template, then this section will look like this:

```
"parameters": {
    "vaultName": {
     "type": "string",
     "defaultValue": "<default-value-of-parameter>"
    },
    "vaultResourceGroup": {
     "type": "string",
     "defaultValue": "<default-value-of-parameter>"
    },
    "secretName": {
     "type": "string",
```

```
        "defaultValue": "<default-value-of-parameter>"
    }
}
```

Behind the `parameters` section, there is a `resource` section in which the key vault reference is defined:

```
"parameters": {
    "adminPassword": {
      "reference": {
          "keyVault": {
                "id": "[resourceId(subscription().
subscriptionId,  parameters('VaultResourceGroup'), 'Microsoft.
KeyVault/vaults', parameters('vaultName'))]"
          },
          "secretName": "[parameters('secretName')]"
      }
    }
}
```

The *linked template* is used for the actual resource deployment. In this file, the local admin username is defined, but the password value is passed from the main template, as follows:

```
"resources": {
"parameters": {
    "adminUsername": {
          "type": "string",
          "defaultValue": "localAdminUsername",
          "metadata": {
                "description": ""
          }
    },
    "adminPassword": {
          "type": "securestring"
    }
}
}
```

Using ARM templates to refer to a key vault secret is a bit more complex, but also works well in DevOps pipelines.

> **Tip**
>
> We have published a complete example of a VM deployment with ARM templates in this book's GitHub repository:
> `https://github.com/PacktPublishing/Mastering-Azure-Security`

You have now learned how to use Azure key vaults and key vault secrets during automated Azure resource deployments with PowerShell, Terraform, and ARM templates. Please make sure that you take a look at this book's GitHub repository, as you will find examples of the steps that we have outlined in this chapter for your reference.

Summary

Azure Key Vault is one of the many services that are underrated but very valuable when it comes to security in Azure. In this chapter, you have learned how to create Azure key vaults and their entities not only with the Azure portal, but also with scripting and deployment languages. You now know how to grant access to an Azure key vault for both individual users and Azure resources and how to reference items that have been securely stored in a key vault.

In the next chapter, we will address data security and encryption, two topics that are heavily dependent on Azure Key Vault, so make sure that you have read and understood this chapter before moving on.

Questions

1. Azure Key Vault is used to secure…

    A. Keys

    B. Secrets

    C. Certificates

    D. All of the above

    E. None of the above

2. How do we control who can access Azure Key Vault information?

    A. Key Vault permissions

    B. Access policies

    C. Conditional access

3. Service-to-service authentication is done via…

    A. Service principal

    B. Certificate

    C. Direct link

4. In order to use Azure Key Vault for **Virtual Machine** (**VM**) deployment, which option do we need to enable?

    A. EnabledForDeployment

    B. EnabledForTemplateDeployment

    C. EnabledForDiskEncryption

5. In order to use Azure Key Vault for **Azure Resource Manager** (**ARM**) deployment, which option do we need to enable?

    A. EnabledForDeployment

    B. EnabledForTemplateDeployment

    C. EnabledForDiskEncryption

6. In order to use Azure Key Vault for VM encryption, which option do we need to enable?

    A. EnabledForDeployment

    B. EnabledForTemplateDeployment

    C. EnabledForDiskEncryption

7. In order to secure secrets during deployment, we need to…

    A. Provide a password

    B. Encrypt a password

    C. Reference an Azure key vault

6
Data Security

Like everything else, data in the cloud must be treated differently to that in on-premises environments. As data is leaving our local environment, and is usually accessible over the internet, we need to be extra careful. We have already mentioned that all data is encrypted at rest, and most communication goes over **HTTPS (Hypertext Transfer Protocol over Secure Socket Layer)** and is encrypted in the move as well. However, there are multiple steps that we can take to ensure additional security and satisfy compliance and different security requirements.

In this chapter, we will be using Azure Key Vault extensively. We've seen how Azure Key Vault can be used for secrets and password management, but we will also see how it can be used to increase data security as well.

We will cover the following topics in this chapter:

- Understanding Azure Storage
- Understanding Azure Virtual Machine disks
- Working on Azure SQL Database

Technical requirements

For this chapter, the following is required:

- PowerShell 5.1, or higher, on Windows (or PowerShell Core 6.x and later on any other platform, including Windows)
- Azure PowerShell modules

- Visual Studio Code
- An Azure subscription

Understanding Azure Storage

Azure Storage is Microsoft's cloud storage service and is highly available, secure, and scalable, plus, it supports a variety of programming languages. It is usually the first data service users encounter when they start using Azure.

All communication inside Azure data centers is over HTTPS, but what happens when we access data from outside? As per the shared responsibility model (explained in *Chapter 1, Azure Security Introduction*), this falls under the user's responsibility. Because of different user requirements, Microsoft does not enforce traffic over HTTPS by default, but there is an option that users can enable to enforce traffic to be encrypted.

Under **Configuration**, there is an option called **Secure transfer required**. To ensure that all traffic is encrypted and over HTTPS, we need to enable this option, as in the following screenshot:

Figure 6.1 – Azure Storage secure transfer

When **Secure transfer required** is enabled, all requests that are not over HTTPS will be rejected, even if they have valid access parameters (such as an access signature or a token). This enhances transfer security by allowing the request to Azure Storage only when coming by a secure connection.

> **Important note**
>
> It's important to remember that Azure Storage does not support HTTPS for custom domain names, so this option does not apply when a custom domain name is used.

Another thing we need to consider is what happens when files are accidentally deleted. This can occur for a number of reasons, such as a user deleting a file by mistake, or numerous applications using the same Azure Storage and one application deleting a file needed by another application. Of course, such situations can be caused by malicious attacks and with intent to cause damage as well. To avoid such situations, we can enable the **Blob soft delete** option under the **Data Protection** setting.

An example is shown in the following screenshot:

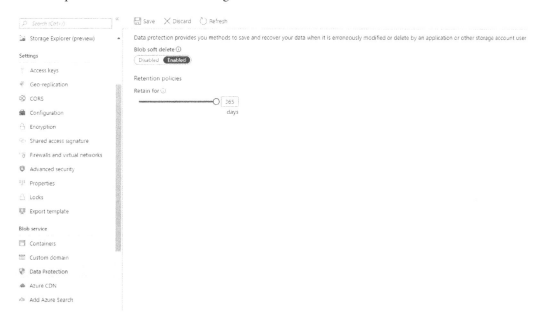

Figure 6.2 – Blob soft delete

Blob soft delete also has retention period settings, which will determine how long files will be saved after they are deleted. These settings can be adjusted to any value between 7 and 365 days. Besides recovering deleted files, **Blob soft delete** enables us to recover previous versions of files, too. If a file is accidentally modified, or we need a previous version of a file for some other reason, **Blob soft delete** can help us to restore the file to any point in time, as long as it's in the timeframe of the effective retention period.

> **Important note**
>
> **Blob soft delete** and the retention period are effective from the moment they are set and cannot be used retroactively. For example, if we discover that we lost a file and then enable this option, it will not help us recover the lost file. To be able to recover files, we need to have the option in place before the incident happens.

Data in Azure is encrypted at rest, and that's no different with Azure Storage. But data is encrypted with Microsoft-managed keys, and this is not always acceptable. In certain situations, caused by compliance and security requirements, we must be in control of keys that are used for encryption. To address such needs, Microsoft has enabled encryption of data with the **Bring Your Own Key (BYOK)** option. The option to use your own key can be enabled under the **Encryption** option, as in the following screenshot:

Figure 6.3 – Azure Storage encryption options

BYOK is enabled by the use of Azure Key Vault, where keys used for storage encryption are stored.

Once we enable **Use your own key**, new settings will appear where we need to provide key vault information. An example is shown in the following screenshot:

Your storage account is currently encrypted with Microsoft managed key by default. You can choose to use your own key.

☑ Use your own key

Encryption key
◯ Enter key URI
◉ Select from Key Vault

Key Vault *
redblue
Select

Encryption key *
MyKey
Select

Figure 6.4 – Storage encryption with a custom key

We can either provide a key **Uniform Resource Identifier** (**URI**), which will contain information about the key vault and key that will be used for encryption, or we can use a second option, which will allow us to select the available key vault and key from a list. Both options will have identical outcomes and the storage will be encrypted. Any new files added to Azure Storage will be encrypted automatically. Any existing files will be retroactively encrypted by a background encryption process, but it will not happen instantly, and the process to encrypt existing data will take time.

Keys in Azure Key Vault can be easily created, but we can also import existing keys from a **Hardware Security Module** (**HSM**). This is for further security and compliance requirements and enables ultimate key management where crypto keys are safeguarded by a dedicated crypt processor.

Encryption in Azure Storage is not only available through the Azure portal, but also through using Azure PowerShell. The following script will create a new Azure Storage account, Key Vault, and key, and then use all the resources provided to encrypt the Azure Storage account that was just created:

```
New-AzResourceGroup -Name 'Packt-Encrypt' -Location 'EastUS'


$storageAccount = Set-AzStorageAccount -ResourceGroupName
'Packt-Encrypt' `
    -Name packtstorageencryption `
    -AssignIdentity


New-AzKeyvault -name 'Pact-KV-01' -ResourceGroupName 'Packt-
Encrypt' `
-Location 'EastUS' `
-EnabledForDiskEncryption `
-EnableSoftDelete `
-EnablePurgeProtection


$KeyVault = Get-AzKeyVault -VaultName 'Pact-KV-01'
-ResourceGroupName 'Packt-Encrypt'


Set-AzKeyVaultAccessPolicy `
    -VaultName $keyVault.VaultName `
    -ObjectId $storageAccount.Identity.PrincipalId `
    -PermissionsToKeys wrapkey,unwrapkey,get,recover
```

```
$key = Add-AzKeyVaultKey -VaultName $keyVault.VaultName -Name
'MyKey' -Destination 'Software'

Set-AzStorageAccount -ResourceGroupName $storageAccount.
ResourceGroupName `
    -AccountName $storageAccount.StorageAccountName `
    -KeyvaultEncryption `
    -KeyName $key.Name `
    -KeyVersion $key.Version `
    -KeyVaultUri $keyVault.VaultUri
```

Another thing we need to consider with Azure Storage is **Advanced Threat Protection** (**ATP**). This option is enabled under **Advanced Security** and it takes our security one step further. It uses security intelligence to detect any threat to our data and provides recommendations in order to increase security.

An example of the **Advanced Threat Protection** blade under the storage account is shown in the following screenshot:

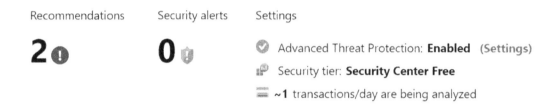

Figure 6.5 – Azure Storage ATP

ATP compares our security settings to the recommended baseline and provides us with additional security options that can be implemented. The second part is to detect unusual and potentially harmful attempts to access or exploit Azure Storage. ATP is closely connected to Azure Security Center, which will be covered in *Chapter 7, Azure Security Center*. But the storage account is not the only Azure service related to storage. Almost every Azure service uses some kind of storage. Among these services, we have Azure **Virtual Machines** (**VMs**) disks, so let's see how can we make these more secure.

Understanding Azure Virtual Machines disks

Azure VM is part of Microsoft's **Infrastructure as a Service** (**IaaS**) offering and is another service that a lot of users encounter early in the cloud journey. Azure VM is usually selected when the user requires more control over the environment than other services can offer. But with more control also comes more responsibility.

Besides network management, which was covered in *Chapter 4, Azure Network Security*, we need to address how we handle data in Azure VM, and by data, we mainly mean disks. Just like all other data, disks for Azure VM are encrypted at rest, and VM uses Azure Service Fabric to securely access content stored on these disks.

But what happens if we decide to download or export a disk used by these machines? Once a disk leaves Azure, it is in an unencrypted state and can be used in any way. This opens certain vulnerabilities that need to be addressed. What if someone gains access to Azure (but does not have access to a VM) and downloads a disk? What if someone decides to back up all disks, but to an unsecure location? These are only a couple of the scenarios that can create serious problems with unauthorized and malicious access to Azure VM disks.

Fortunately, we have the option to use Azure Key Vault and enable the further encryption of disks. Disks encrypted in this way will stay encrypted even after they are exported, downloaded, or leave an Azure data center in any way.

If we go to Azure VM and take a look at our disks, we can see that, by default, disk encryption is not enabled. An example is shown in the following screenshot:

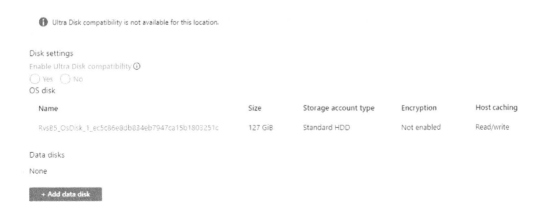

Figure 6.6 – Azure VM disk options to encrypt disks

We need to use Azure Key Vault and we need the key to be stored in the key vault.

We can use Azure PowerShell to enable disk encryption for Azure VM disks. A sample script is provided here:

```
New-AzResourceGroup -Name "Packt-Encrypt" -Location "EastUS"

$cred = Get-Credential

New-AzVM -Name 'Packt-VM-01' `
-Credential $cred `
-ResourceGroupName 'Packt-Encrypt' `
-Image win2016datacenter `
-Size Standard_D2S_V3

New-AzKeyvault -name 'Pact-KV-01' `
-ResourceGroupName 'Packt-Encrypt' `
-Location EastUS `
-EnabledForDiskEncryption `
-EnableSoftDelete `
-EnablePurgeProtection

$KeyVault = Get-AzKeyVault -VaultName 'Pact-KV-01'
-ResourceGroupName 'Packt-Encrypt'

Set-AzVMDiskEncryptionExtension -ResourceGroupName 'Packt-
Encrypt' `
-VMName 'Packt-VM-01' `
-DiskEncryptionKeyVaultUrl $KeyVault.VaultUri `
-DiskEncryptionKeyVaultId $KeyVault.ResourceId

Get-AzVmDiskEncryptionStatus -VMName Packt-VM-01
-ResourceGroupName Packt-Encrypt
```

This script creates a new Azure VM, a new key vault, and a new key. The created resources are then used to enable disk encryption for the just-created Azure VM. Finally, we can check the status of the disk and verify whether it was successfully encrypted. We can verify that the disk is encrypted in the Azure portal, as shown in the following screenshot:

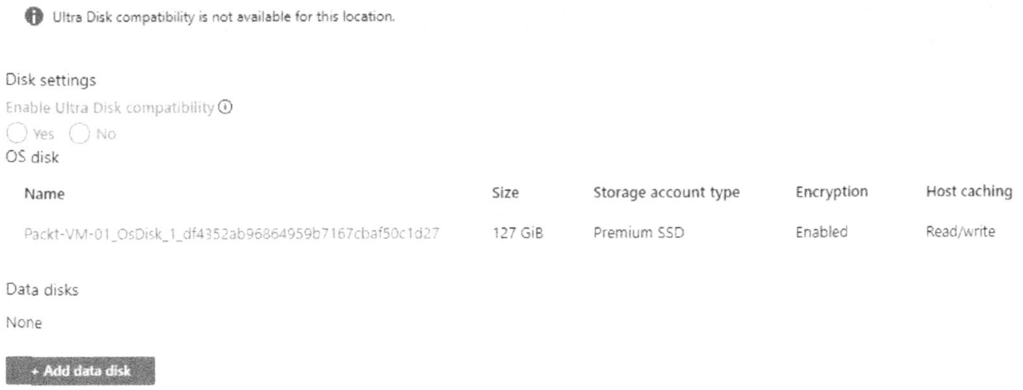

Figure 6.7– Azure VM portal

The Azure VM disk is not encrypted: it can be accessed, used to create a new VM (Azure or a local Hyper-V), or attached to an existing VM. Encrypting the disk will prevent such access, unless the user has access to the key vault that was used during the encryption process.

Working on Azure SQL Database

Azure SQL Database is Microsoft's relational database cloud offering, which falls under the platform as a service model, often referred to as **Database as a Service** (**DBaaS**). It's highly available and provides a high-performance data storage layer. Because of that, it's often the choice when it comes to selecting a database in the cloud.

There is a whole section of security-related features in Azure SQL Database's settings. There are four different options:

- **ADVANCED DATA SECURITY**

- **AUDITING**

- **DYNAMIC DATA MASKING**

- **TRANSPARENT DATA ENCRYPTION**

If we enable **ADVANCED DATA SECURITY**, we get a few advantages:

- **VULNERABILITY ASSESSMENT SETTINGS**

- **ADVANCED THREAT PROTECTION SETTINGS**

- **DATA DISCOVERY & CLASSIFICATION**

The options to enable **ADVANCED DATA SECURITY** are shown in the following screenshot:

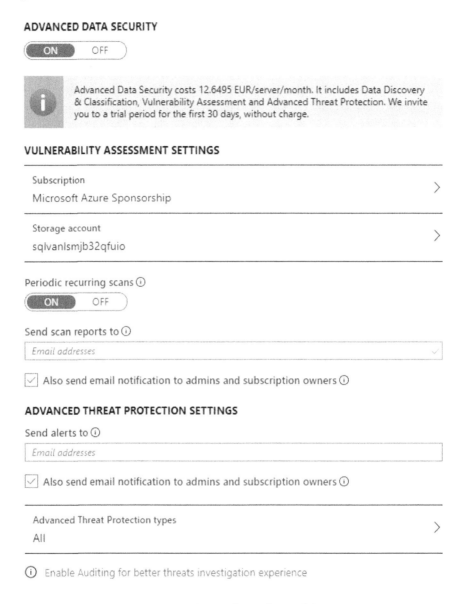

Figure 6.8 – Azure SQL Database advanced data security

Each of these options has additional configurations, which we need to set before using **ADVANCED DATA SECURITY**:

1. **VULNERABILITY ASSESSMENT SETTINGS** requires Azure Storage, which is where data will be kept and will provide security recommendations based on the current status. The assessment will be performed manually, and we can select whether the report will be sent to specific users or to all admins and subscription owners. The assessment report has the following format:

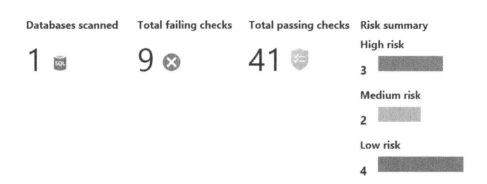

Figure 6.9 – Azure SQL Database assessment results

The vulnerability assessment compares our current settings to the baseline and provides a list of checks that are not satisfied. It also provides a classification of checks based on risk level: **High risk**, **Medium risk**, and **Low risk**.

2. **ADVANCED THREAT PROTECTION SETTINGS** is very similar to this option in Azure Storage: it detects anything unusual and potentially harmful. We have a couple of additional settings compared to Azure Storage: we can select what types of threats we want to detect and define who gets notifications if a threat is detected.

A list of threats we can monitor is shown in the following diagram:

Figure 6.10 – Azure SQL Database advanced threat protection settings

Similar to **VULNERABILITY ASSESSMENT SETTINGS**, notifications about threats can be sent to specific users or all admins and subscription owners.

3. The final option under **ADVANCED DATA SECURITY** is **DATA DISCOVERY & CLASSIFICATION**. This option carries out data assessment and provides a classification for any data that should be confidential. Assessments are carried out based on various compliance and security requirements, and data is classified as confidential based on one or more criteria. For example, we may have some user information that should be classified based on the **General Data Protection Regulation (GDPR)**. But among user information, we may have social security or credit card numbers that are classified by many other compliance requirements. **DATA DISCOVERY & CLASSIFICATION** only provides information about classified data types, but it's up to the user to decide what to proceed with and how to do so.

This brings us to the next security setting under Azure SQL Database – **Dynamic Data Masking**. In the past, we could provide the user with access to different layers, such as database, schema, table, or row. However, we could not provide access based on the column. **Dynamic Data Masking** changes this and enables us to provide user access to a table but mask certain columns that the user should not be able to access.

For example, let's say that we want to provide access to a customer table, but the user should not be able to access the customer's email address. We can create masking on the email column, and the user will be able to see all the information except the masked column, which will be displayed as masked (there are default masks for common data types, but custom masks can be created). For masked columns, we can exclude certain users. All administrators are excluded by default and cannot be excluded. An example of **Dynamic Data Masking** is shown in the following screenshot:

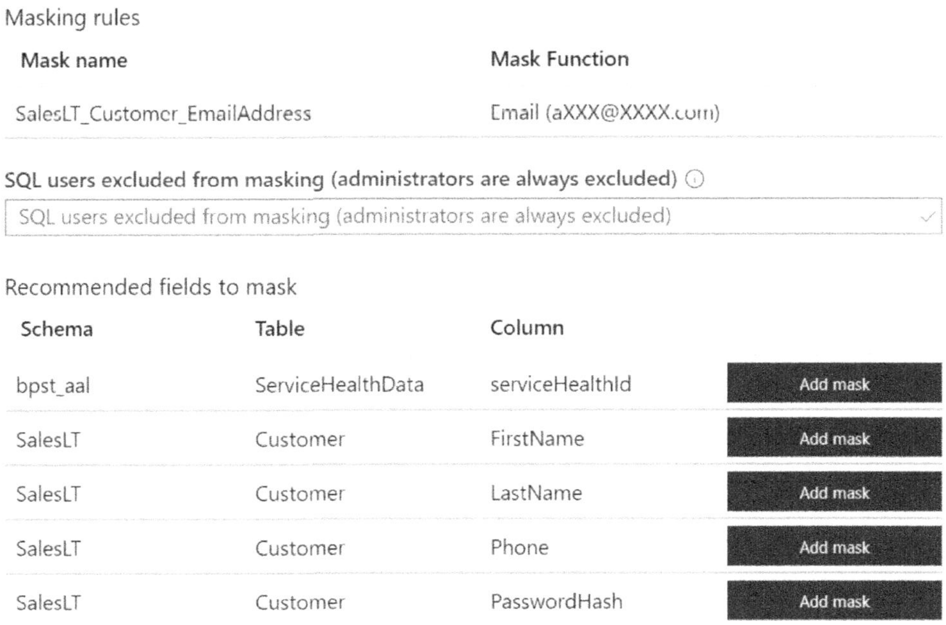

Masking rules

Mask name	Mask Function
SalesLT_Customer_EmailAddress	Email (aXXX@XXXX.com)

SQL users excluded from masking (administrators are always excluded) ⓘ

SQL users excluded from masking (administrators are always excluded)   ✓

Recommended fields to mask

Schema	Table	Column	
bpst_aal	ServiceHealthData	serviceHealthId	Add mask
SalesLT	Customer	FirstName	Add mask
SalesLT	Customer	LastName	Add mask
SalesLT	Customer	Phone	Add mask
SalesLT	Customer	PasswordHash	Add mask

Figure 6.11 – Dynamic Data Masking

Dynamic Data Masking is connected to **DATA DISCOVERY & CLASSIFICATION**. The user will receive data masking recommendations based on information provided by **DATA DISCOVERY & CLASSIFICATION**.

The **Auditing** option enables us to define where various logs will be stored. There are three different options available:

- **Storage**
- **Log Analytics**
- **Event Hubs**

As many regulatory and security compliance standards require access and event logs to be stored, this option enables us to not only keep logs for auditing purposes but also to help us to understand and trace events whenever needed. Auditing can be enabled for a single database or on a server level. In the case that server auditing is enabled, logs will be kept for all databases located on that server.

The last security setting under Azure SQL Database is **Transparent Database Encryption (TDE)**. TDE is a method of encrypting data at rest and performs real-time encryption and decryption of data and log files at the page level. It uses a **Database Encryption Key (DEK)** to encrypt data, associated backups, and transactional logs.

For older databases, this setting is not enabled, the TDE status is **OFF**, and **Encryption status** is **Unencrypted**. An example of this is shown in the following screesnhot:

Figure 6.12 – Azure SQL Database TDE settings

For newer databases, TDE is already on and the encryption status is encrypted, as shown in the following screenshot:

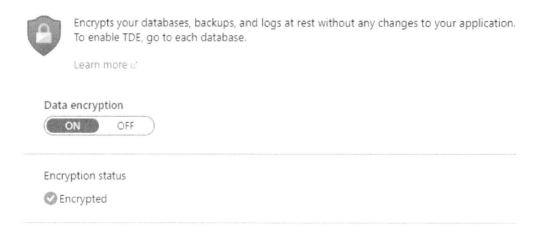

Figure 6.13 – Azure SQL Database encrypted with TDE

We will get the same effect by switching TDE on for older databases. However, this method uses Microsoft-provided keys for encryption. If we need to follow regulatory and security compliance standards and manage keys ourselves, we must turn to Azure **Key Vault** once again. To enable TDE with our own key from Azure **Key Vault**, we must enable this setting at the server level. Under TDE settings, under **Server**, we can turn **Use your own key** on, as in the following screenshot:

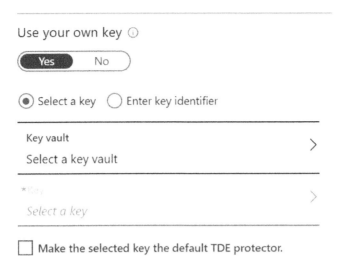

Figure 6.14 – Using a custom key for TDE

Once we turn this option on, we need to provide the key vault and key that will be used. Optionally, we can set the selected key to be the default TDE protector.

Enabling the option to use the key from the key vault for TDE will not enable TDE on every database located on the selected server. TDE must be enabled for each database separately. If this option is not set on the server, enabling TDE on the database will use Microsoft-managed keys. If the option is enabled on the server level, enabling TDE on the database will use the key from the key vault that is defined.

Encryption can be set using Azure PowerShell, as in the following sample script:

1. We need to define parameters for execution. These will be used across the entire script, basically in each and every command we execute:

```
$RGName = 'Packt-Encrypt'
$servername = 'packtSQL'
$DBName = 'test'
```

2. Next we need to log in to our Azure subscription:

```
$cred = Get-Credential
```

3. We will create Resource group, Azure SQL Server and Azure SQL database.

```
$RG = New-AzResourceGroup -Name $RGName -Location
'EastUS'
```

```
$server = Set-AzSqlServer -ResourceGroupName $RG.
ResourceGroupName `

-ServerName $servername `

-AssignIdentity


$server = New-AzSqlServer -ResourceGroupName $RG.
ResourceGroupName  `

-Location 'EastUS' `

-ServerName $server.ServerName `

-ServerVersion "12.0" `

-SqlAdministratorCredentials $cred `

-AssignIdentity

$database = New-AzSqlDatabase  -ResourceGroupName $RG.
ResourceGroupName `

-ServerName $server.ServerName `

-DatabaseName $DBName `

-RequestedServiceObjectiveName "S0" `

-SampleName "AdventureWorksLT"
```

4. Next, we need to create the Azure Key vault, which will be used in the data encryption process:

```
New-AzKeyvault -name 'Pact-KV-01' -ResourceGroupName $RG.
ResourceGroupName`

-Location 'EastUS' `

-EnabledForDiskEncryption `

-EnableSoftDelete `

-EnablePurgeProtection


$KeyVault = Get-AzKeyVault -VaultName 'Pact-KV-01' `

-ResourceGroupName $RG.ResourceGroupName
```

5. We now need to set the key vault access policy to enable encryption and add a key that will be used to encrypt the data:

```
Set-AzKeyVaultAccessPolicy `

-VaultName $keyVault.VaultName `

-ObjectId $storageAccount.Identity.PrincipalId `
```

```
-PermissionsToKeys wrapkey,unwrapkey,get,recover

$key = Add-AzKeyVaultKey -VaultName $keyVault.VaultName `
-Name 'MyKey' `
-Destination 'Software'
```

6. Finally, we assign a key to Azure SQL Server, enable TDE using custom key from Key Vault, and encrypt the database using that key:

```
Add-AzSqlServerKeyVaultKey -ResourceGroupName $RG.
ResourceGroupName   `
-ServerName $server.ServerName `
-KeyId $key.Id

Set-AzSqlServerTransparentDataEncryptionProtector
-ResourceGroupName $RG.ResourceGroupName    `
-ServerName $server.ServerName `
-Type AzureKeyVault `
-KeyId $key.Id

Get-AzSqlServerTransparentDataEncryptionProtector
-ResourceGroupName $RG.ResourceGroupName    `
-ServerName $server.ServerName

Set-AzSqlDatabaseTransparentDataEncryption
-ResourceGroupName -ResourceGroupName $RG.
ResourceGroupName   `
-ServerName $server.ServerName `
-DatabaseName $database.DatabaseName `
-State "Enabled"
```

If the database has TDE enabled, with Microsoft-managed keys, enabling our own key from the key vault on a server level will not automatically transfer the encryption from the managed key to our own key. We must perform decryption and enable encryption again to use the key from the key vault.

Summary

With all this work on the network and identity levels, we still need to do more and encrypt our data in the cloud. But is that enough? Often it is not, and then we find ourselves needing to do even more. Threats are becoming more and more sophisticated, and we need to find ways of increasing our security. In this chapter, we briefly mentioned Azure Security Center. It may be the one thing that can give us an advantage in creating a secure cloud environment and stopping threats and attacks before they even happen.

In the next chapter, we will discuss how Azure Security Center uses security intelligence to be a central security safeguard in Azure.

Questions

1. What will the **Secure transfer required** option do?

   A. Enforce data encryption

   B. Enforce HTTPS

   C. Enforce FTPS

2. To protect data from accidental deletion, what needs to be enabled?

   A. Data protection

   B. Recycle Bin

   C. Blob soft delete

3. Is data in Azure Storage encrypted by default?

   A. Yes

   B. No

4. Are Azure **Virtual Machine** (**VM**) disks encrypted by default?

    A. Yes

    B. No

5. Is Azure SQL Database encrypted by default?

    A. Yes

    B. No

6. Data in Azure can be encrypted with…

    A. Microsoft-provided keys

    B. User-provided keys

    C. Both of the above

7. Data in Azure SQL Database can be restricted using…

    A. Data Classification

    B. Dynamic Data Masking

    C. Transparent Database Encryption (TDE)

Section 3:
Security
Management

In this section, you will learn how to monitor security in Microsoft Azure, apply recommendations, and detect threats before they happen.

This section comprises the following chapters:

7
Azure Security Center

Azure Security Center is meant to be that one tool that gives you a unified overview of your hybrid cloud environment's current security configuration, and informs you about current threats and attacks against your services.

In this chapter, we will cover the following topics:

- Introducing Azure Security Center
- Secure score and recommendations
- Automating responses
- Just-in-time access for Azure Virtual Machines
- Advanced Cloud Defense

Introducing Azure Security Center

With cloud computing the main paradigm in the modern IT world, there are many benefits that come with this new way of working. IT is no longer an end in itself and employees are way more productive than they were back in the day. But there are also new challenges when it comes to protecting modern IT environments.

In *Chapter 3, Managing Cloud Identities*, we already covered advanced identity protection and that it is no longer enough to protect network boundaries, however, there are some other main security challenges that come with cloud computing.

How can you make sure you protect your ever-changing cloud services and applications? This is one of the value propositions of cloud computing and, in fact, probably the main benefit is that you can easily change and adapt in cloud environments. Be it **Define acronym continuous integration (CI)/ continuous delivery (CD), Virtual Machine (VM).** Define acronym upscaling, or service decommissioning, cloud environments are dynamically changing. But at the same time, one of the main challenges is to keep track of these changes and to make sure that a company's services always adhere to their security baseline.

The threat landscape is evolving, and attacks are becoming increasingly sophisticated. Bad actors are using attack automation and evasion techniques, and at the same time, they are leveraging tools that help them to conduct attacks across the cyber kill chain. So, they no longer need to be highly trained technology experts, which results in an increasing number of sophisticated attacks, some of which are spear-phishing and credential theft attacks. Also, attackers are using hijacked computers, tied to bot networks, to conduct widely spread password spray attacks, which can be hard to recognize.

We need human expertise, creativity, and adaptability to combat human threat actors. The downside is that security skills are in short supply. Currently, there are about 3 million open positions in the cyber security sector out there worldwide, with that number increasing. This includes not only cyber threat hunters, but also security engineers and administrators with a focus on managing internal IT systems.

Azure Security Center is a service that offers two main solutions:

1. As a **Cloud Security Posture Management (CSPM)** solution, Azure Security Center constantly provides information about the current configuration status of all your cloud resources to avoid misconfiguration with regard to security.

2. As a **Cloud Workload Protection Platform** (**CWPP**), Azure Security Center provides protection against cyber threats aimed at servers, no matter whether they are running in Microsoft Azure, on premises, or in another cloud platform, as well as protection against threats aimed at your cloud-native workloads in Azure, for example key vaults, storage accounts, SQL databases, and more:

Figure. 7.1 – Azure Security Center Overview dashboard

The central Azure Security Center **Overview** dashboard is divided into three different areas:

- **Policy & compliance**
- **Resource security hygiene**
- **Threat protection**

In the **Policy & compliance** section, you'll find information about everything related to *compliance* and *governance*. For example, **Subscription coverage** gives you insights into the enrollment state of Azure Security Center over all your subscriptions. In other words, you can see whether there are Azure subscriptions in your tenant that are not covered by Azure Security Center. You also get a view of your **Overall secure score**, a number that reflects how well (or badly) your environment is protected. **Regulatory compliance**, finally, is a part of Azure Security Center that will help you to make sure that your cloud environment is compliant regarding regulations such as **Azure CIS 1.1.0** and **ISO27001**.

The second section in Azure Security Center, **Resource security hygiene**, is the area that shows you recommendations regarding your current security configuration. By continuously assessing your environmental configuration, Azure Security Center gives you recommendations regarding security best practices to help you protect your environments.

In the **Threat protection** section, the last of the three main sections, Azure Security Center shows you current security alerts and incidents (which are cumulations of single alerts that are brought into context):

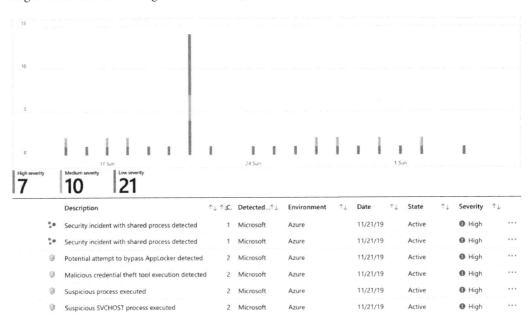

Figure. 7.2 – Security alerts and incidents

You can select an incident or an alert to get more information about the context and about remediation steps for every single alert and can trigger an Azure logic app as a response for the alert. For example, you could create a logic app that sends out an email or a post to a Microsoft Teams channel.

> **Note:**
> Azure Security Center is a tool for security engineers and administrators that are responsible for protecting (hybrid) enterprise infrastructures. It is a tool that helps in implementing security best practices and gives a security overview. For threat hunting and digging deeper into alerts and incidents, you would be better off using Azure Sentinel, a SIEM/SOAR solution that we will talk about in *Chapter 8, Azure Sentinel*.

Now, that you have gotten a quick overview of Azure Security Center and its **Overview** dashboard, let's dig a bit deeper and see how it technically works.

Enabling Azure Security Center

As a first step in leveraging Azure Security Center, we must enable this service and provide initial configuration parameters. There are several key components we need to consider before starting.

Azure Security Center basically relies on Azure Log Analytics and its respective workspace, on Intelligent Security Graph, and on Azure Policy:

- The **Log Analytics workspace** is used for storing all kinds of log information, such as Windows Server security event logs, or Linux server syslog entries, but also for storing security alerts and other information.

- **Intelligent Security Graph** is an AI/ML-based backend used to identify attacks and threats by evaluating the billions of threats signals that are generated in Microsoft products and services every day. Alerts and incidents in the **Threat Protection** section of Azure Security Center are basically generated using Intelligent Security Graph (and tools that rely on it and integrate into Azure Security Center, such as Microsoft Defender ATP).

- **Azure Policy**, a service we have already covered in *Chapter 2, Governance and Security*, is what recommendations in Azure Security Center rely on.

Azure Security Center comes in two different pricing tiers:

- Free
- Standard

With the free tier of Azure Security Center, you get access to your Azure Secure Score, as well as continuous assessments of your current configuration and security recommendations for Azure resources. If you want to also protect on-premise servers or VMs running in another public cloud platform, or if you want to leverage other features, such as just-in-time VM access, adaptive application controls and network hardening, the regulatory compliance dashboards, threat protection, and so on, you need to enable the standard tier of Azure Security Center.

Standard tier pricing depends on the resources you protect and is calculated as follows:

- VMs and servers: $15 per node per month
- Azure App Service: $15 per instance per month
- PaaS SQL Servers: $15 per server per month
- Storage Accounts: $0.02 per 10,000 storage transactions
- SQL Server on VMs: Free (during preview)
- Container Registries: $0.29 per container image (preview pricing)
- Azure K8s Service: $2 per VM core per month (preview pricing)

> **Important note**
>
> Even for the free tier of Azure Security Center, pricing for Azure Log Analytics applies. This is also true for the standard tier of Azure Security Center, where Log Analytics pricing is calculated in addition to the ASC standard tier cost mentioned above. Preview pricing is subject to change after the respective services become **generally available (GA)**.

Before you can start using Azure Security Center, you must define which pricing tier you want to use per Azure subscription and connect Azure Security Center to a Log Analytics workspace. You do so by navigating to the Azure **Security Center** portal and selecting **Pricing & settings**, where you can define the pricing tier and other global settings per Azure subscription:

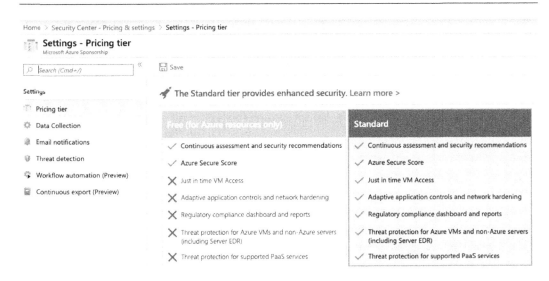

Figure. 7.3 – Selecting an Azure Security Center pricing tier

In the **Data Collection** area, you can configure **Auto Provisioning,** which enables the automatic installation of the Microsoft Monitoring Agent:

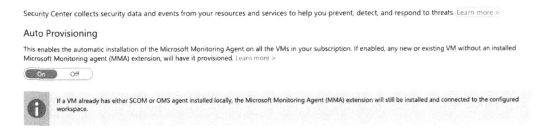

Figure. 7.4 – Enabling Auto Provisioning

You need to also define whether you want to use a default Log Analytics workspace, which is automatically created by Azure Security Center, or whether you want to use an existing workspace:

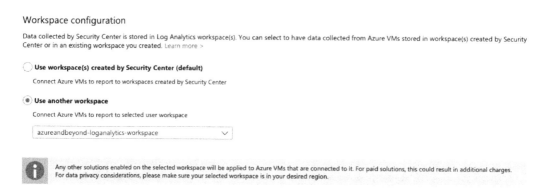

Figure. 7.5 – Selecting your Log Analytics workspace configuration

The last decision you have to make in this section is about the amount of security and the number of AppLocker event log files you want to submit to the configured Log Analytics workspace. You can choose between the following options:

- **None**
- **Minimal**
- **Common**
- **All Events**

After Azure Security Center is enabled, we can start benefitting from all the advantages it offers and make Azure security better. But Azure Security Center is not limited to cloud resources and can be extended to on-premises resources as well. Next, we will look at tools that Azure Security Center provides that enable us to increase our security posture.

Azure Secure Score and recommendations

Like several other services in the Microsoft enterprise cloud, such as Azure AD, and Office 365, Azure Security Center now also offers a security gamification option, the **Azure Secure Score**. The idea is to show the number of points you could achieve at a maximum for your currently deployed Azure resources and what your current secure score is. The more points you get, the better your security posture is. It's like bringing the complexity of cloud security down to a simple game:

Secure Score Dashboard

Figure. 7.6 – Azure Secure Score Dashboard

The **Secure Score Dashboard** offers you an overview of your current **Overall secure score** and your **Secure score by category**. If you click one of the Secure Score categories, you will see recommendations within that category with their respective Secure Score impact. The higher a recommendation's Secure Score impact is, the more important it is to remediate the corresponding misconfiguration.

> **Tip**
> Secure Score does not reflect industry-standard security benchmarks; for example, more than 700 out of 1,000 points is secure and less than 300 is extremely unprotected. Secure Score will only calculate points you can achieve depending on your currently deployed resources and regarding recommendations that already have been met, just like in a game.

Two Azure environments are never comparable regarding their secure scores. You can only say that the more points you achieve, the better it is. If you compare Figure. *7.1: Azure Security Center overview dashboard* and figure. *7.6: Azure Secure Score Dashboard*, you'll realize that the overall secure scores do not match (393 of 655 versus 350 of 640). These screenshots show the same Azure environment with 6 days in between. There have been some resources that were deleted in the meantime, but no other configuration changes occurred. Azure Secure Score can be used to compare security levels for the same environment at different points in time. Every change in your cloud configuration will have an impact on the overall secure score and Azure Secure Score is directly connected with recommendations. So, the more recommendations you meet, the better your secure score will be. Now, let's move on to recommendations and see what is provided there.

Working with recommendations

In *Chapter 2, Governance and Security*, you already learned that monitoring is essential in terms of security and how to leverage policies to create guardrails for your Azure environment. The nice thing about Azure Security Center is that its free tier is automatically enabled once you visit the **Azure Security Center** dashboard in the Azure portal and security policies, continuous security assessments, and recommendations that help you protect your Azure resources are automatically included. These recommendations are security best practices that can be enabled or disabled in your security policy, which relies on the Azure Policy service you learned about in *Chapter 2, Governance and Security*. Every recommendation refers to an audit policy, and if a resource is non-compliant regarding a particular policy, the **Recommendation** dashboard will reflect this failed resource:

Recommendation	Secure Score Impact ↑↓	Failed Resources ↑↓	Severity ↑↓
MFA should be enabled on accounts with owner permissions on your subscription	+50	3 of 3 subscriptions	
Subnets should be associated with a Network Security Group	+30	2 of 2 subnets	
Vulnerability assessment solution should be installed on your virtual machines	+30	3 of 5 virtual mach...	
Vulnerabilities in security configuration on your machines should be remediated	+30	5 of 5 virtual mach...	
System updates should be installed on your machines	+24	4 of 5 virtual mach...	
Adaptive Application Controls should be enabled on virtual machines	+20	4 of 5 virtual mach...	
Just-In-Time network access control should be applied on virtual machines	+18	3 of 5 virtual mach...	
Install endpoint protection solution on virtual machines	+15	4 of 5 virtual mach...	
Secure transfer to storage accounts should be enabled Quick Fix!	+13	7 of 11 storage ac...	

Figure. 7.7 – Failed resources in the Azure Security Center Recommendation dashboard

When you click one of the recommendations, you'll see a description and threats this recommendation protects from. Depending on the recommendation, you can either remediate it directly from Azure Security Center, or you'll be informed about manual remediation steps. The **Quick Fix!** button from the preceding screenshot enables single-click remediation for several recommendations, one of which is disabling insecure connectivity to all of your storage accounts.

The Azure Security Center community

This section, in the **Azure Security Center (ASC)**, blade, contains some very useful links that can help you expand your usage of Azure Security Center. On the community forum, you can check for various announcements, ask questions, or look for previously posted questions. The community blog offers detailed descriptions on some topics and how-to guides. User Voice offers you the chance to ask for new features or improvements.

One of the useful links in the Azure Security Center community section is to the Azure Security Center GitHub repository. The repository contains security recommendations that are still in preview, Azure Policy custom definition for at-scale management, Logic Apps templates for automated responses (alerting or auto-heal), and security remediations in the form of programmatic tools and PowerShell scripts. This is a community repository, so everyone has the chance to contribute. If you've authored templates, scripts, or something else, and you think they may be helpful to others, feel free to submit them.

Workflow automation and sections in Azure Security Center

Before we start with workflow automation, we need to quickly explain what logic apps are.

Azure Logic Apps is a cloud service that helps you to schedule, automate, and orchestrate different tasks, processes, and workflows. It also offers the ability to integrate with different applications, datasets, systems, and services across organizations. This makes it very useful in a number of scenarios, whether you want to create a repetitive automated task, trigger an action whenever a condition happens, or connect different systems.

In terms of using Logic Apps with Azure Security Center, we can use workflow automation in order to set up a logic app to respond to Azure Security Center alerts. Alerts can be separated into groups, threats, and recommendations. Based on alerts, we can define an automated response based on severity and type.

For example, we can set up a logic app to be automatically triggered whenever a brute-force attack is detected in Azure Security Center. We need to create a workflow that will automatically trigger a logic app based on the detected threat, as shown in the following screenshot:

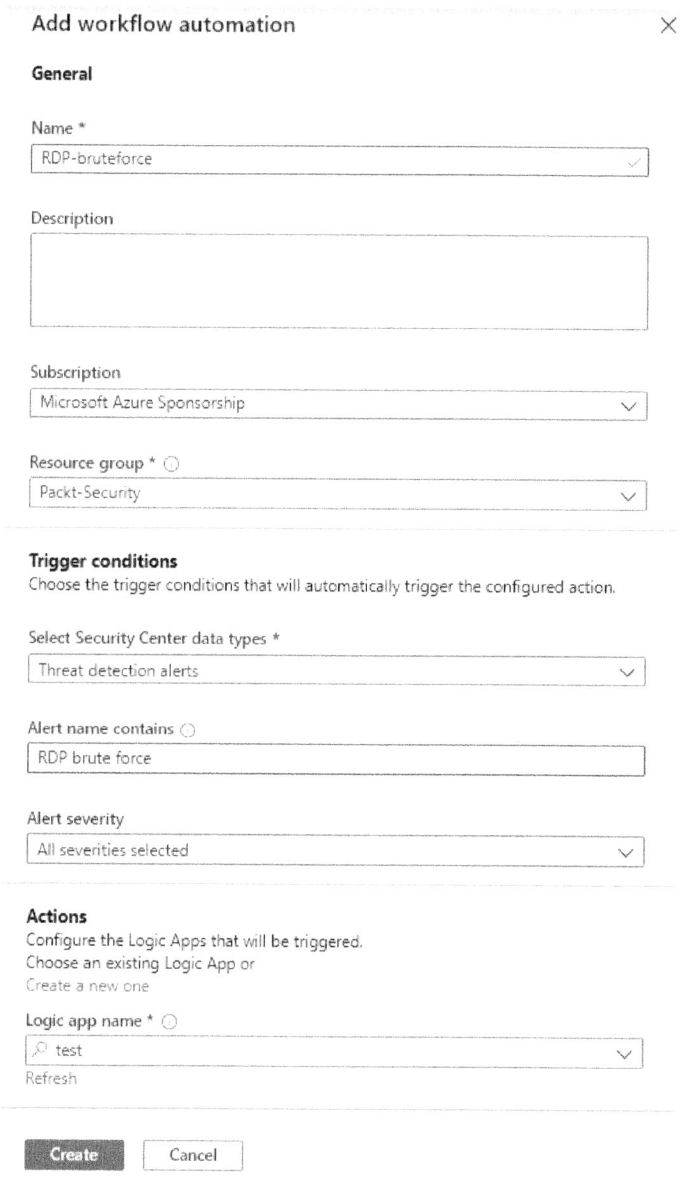

Add workflow automation   ✕

General

Name *

RDP-bruteforce

Description

Subscription

Microsoft Azure Sponsorship

Resource group *

Packt-Security

Trigger conditions
Choose the trigger conditions that will automatically trigger the configured action.

Select Security Center data types *

Threat detection alerts

Alert name contains

RDP brute force

Alert severity

All severities selected

Actions
Configure the Logic Apps that will be triggered.
Choose an existing Logic App or
Create a new one

Logic app name *

🔍 test

Refresh

Create   Cancel

Figure. 7.8 – Configuring a logic app trigger in workflow automation

This will only set up a trigger for the specified logic app. We'll still need to configure a logic app for the response. For example, we could send a notification that a brute-force attack has been detected. Logic apps have many connectors configured and we can set up any or more of them. Some options are to send email notifications or to post messages in a Teams group:

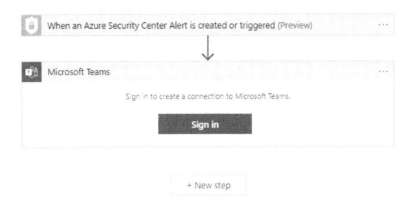

Figure. 7.9 – Configuring an alert to be posted in a Teams channel

This is only one example of what an automated response could be. We can set up a number of custom actions such as temporarily disabling access to an attacked resource or blocking access for IP addresses from which an attack originates. The Azure Security Center GitHub repository offers a number of templates and scripts that can be used to automate a response.

Policy & compliance

The section covering policy and compliance contains four subsections:

- Coverage
- Secure score
- Security policy
- Regulatory compliance

The coverage and secure score sections offer a security overview per subscription. The coverage section shows information about which Azure Security Center plan is enabled on each individual subscription and how many resources are covered per subscription. The secure score section can be seen on the main dashboard but this time it offers per-subscription information, showing us the score for each individual subscription.

The security policy section helps you define what kind of security recommendations will be sent by Azure Security Center. By default, recommendations will be made based on the most common compliance standards and custom Azure CIS. This can be done on the subscription level, and we can set different settings for different subscriptions.

Examples of default settings are shown in the following screenshot:

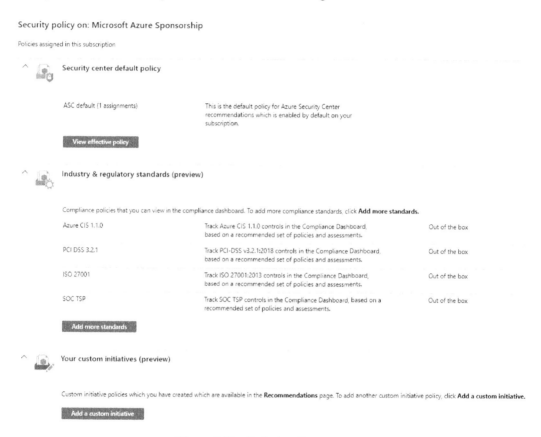

Figure. 7.10 – Default policy settings

Standard policies that are enabled by default are Azure CIS 1.1.0, PCI DSS 3.2.1, ISO 27001, and SOC TSP. Additional industry and regulatory standards that are available are NIST SP 800-53 R4, UK Official and UK NHS, Canada Federal PBMM, and SWIFT CSP CSCF v2020.

Besides industry and regulatory standards, we can create custom policies that apply to our organization. Using custom policies, we can track what happens in our Azure environment, based on special requirements. To create a custom policy, we need to define a subscription to which this will apply and select definitions that we want to track. For example, we can set a policy to track whether SQL-managed instances have Transparent data encryption (TDE) enabled with custom keys, or whether Azure Backup is enabled for Azure Virtual Machines. Azure Security Center will the track resources on a defined subscription and send notifications when policies are not applied. It's important to mention that this will only track and send notifications that resources are not compliant with the policy. We need to act and make changes to recommendations to actually change the state of the resource and comply.

An example of a custom policy is shown in the following screenshot:

BASICS

Definition location *

Microsoft Azure Sponsorship

Name * ⓘ

Enter the name for your initiative

Description ⓘ

Describe the initiative you are authoring

Category ⓘ

◉ Create new   ◯ Use existing

Category

Initiative parameters ⓘ

Parameter name	Display name	Type	Allowed values

Figure. 7.11 – Creating a custom security policy

With security policies, we can define which (if any) industry standards we want to be compliant with. Under regulatory compliance, we can see how our subscription holds when evaluated on each standard. Four standards are currently available: Azure CIS 1.1.0, PCI DSS 3.2.1, ISO 27001, and SOC TSP. Each standard has controls, and we can see which controls are passed or failed. There are a total of 330 controls that intervene between standards. The regulatory compliance section offers an overview of all the controls and controls for each individual standard, as shown in the following screenshot:

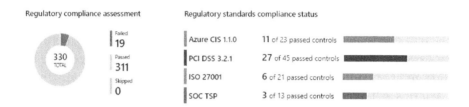

Figure. 7.12 – Regulatory compliance overview

For each available standard, we can see a more detailed report with information on passed and failed controls. Similar to recommendations, we have a list of actions that need to be taken to pass controls. And the same as with recommendations, actions can be presented in the form of instructions that we need to perform manually, or they can offer a quick fix to resolve issues.

An example of failed controls is shown in the following screenshot:

Figure. 7.13 – Regulatory compliance overview

Controls are there only as a guideline; they are not fixed automatically. A list of failed controls is there as a reminder of what needs to be addressed and fixed in order to pass controls.

Resource security hygiene

This section offers a different view of Azure Security Center recommendations. The section is divided into the following subsections:

- **Recommendations**
- **Compute & Apps**
- **Networking**
- **IoT hub & resources**
- **Data & storage**
- **Identity & access**
- **Security solutions**

The **Recommendations** section offers the same information as seen in the overview, and the rest of the subsections offer subcategories based on types. For example, the **Networking** subsection will provide only recommendations referring to Azure network services, such as network security groups, network interfaces, virtual networks, and so on.

The last subsection, **Security solutions**, enables the integration of third-party tools with Azure Security Center. We can add non-Azure servers to be monitored by Azure Security Center, send Azure Security Center logs to SIEM, or add a web application firewall or next-generation firewall.

A lot of companies and organizations require a central logging solution – **SIEM (Security Information and Event Management)**. All products and systems that have custom logging and a centralized solution that helps you identify events across an organization are very useful. So, the ability to send information and logs gathered by Azure Security Center may be a very important requirement, especially for large organizations and enterprises. Some SIEM solutions that may be integrated with Azure Security Center are IBM QRadar, Splunk, SumoLogic, ArcSight, Syslog server, LogRhythm, and Logz.io.

The option to add non-Azure Virtual Machines to Azure Security Center enables true hybrid-cloud capabilities. The security enhancements that Azure Security Center enables for Azure Virtual Machines can be extended to basically any other server, running in a local data center or another cloud. This allows advanced threat detection and alerts and incident investigation across our environment.

Advanced cloud defense

Advanced cloud defense presents additional tooling for enhanced threat mitigation. Four additional tools are available:

- Adaptive application controls
- Just-in-time VM access
- Adaptive network hardening
- File integrity monitoring

Adaptive application controls enable you to have control over which applications can run on servers protected by Azure Security Center. This applies both to Azure and non-Azure VMs and servers. We can control what can run on servers by allowing only specific applications or types of applications to run and prevent any malicious or unauthorized software. We can create different groups that will track the file type protection based on location, operating system, and environment type. Servers can be added to multiple groups to track different protection modes. An example of a group to protect a Windows VM in Azure, located in the US region with the audit option for any EXE, MSI, or script, is shown in the following screenshot:

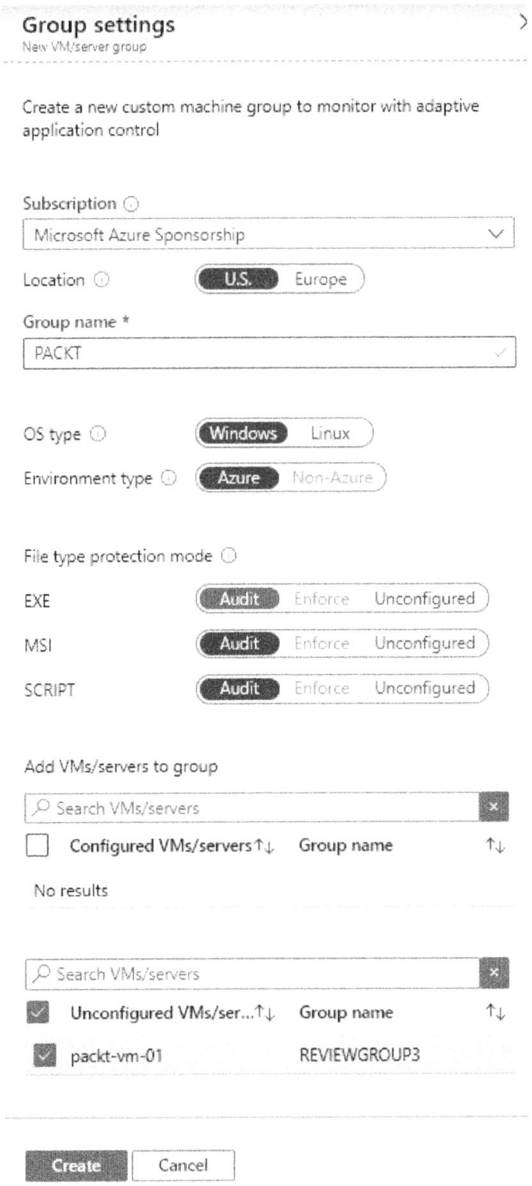

Figure. 7.14 – Adaptive application control group settings

Azure Virtual Machine management is another topic that needs to be taken very seriously. Best practice is to perform any management tasks only over a secure connection, using a P2S or S2S connection. An alternative is to use one VM as a jumpbox, and then perform management from there. But even in this situation, the connection must be secure.

Just-in-time VM access

Just-in-time access for Azure Virtual Machines is used to block inbound traffic to VMs until specific traffic is temporarily allowed. This reduces their exposure to attacks by narrowing down the surface and enabling access. Enabling **Just In Time** (**JIT**) will block inbound traffic on all ports that are usually used for management, such as RDP, SSH, or WinRM. The user must explicitly request access, which will be granted for a period of time but only for a known IP address. This approach is the same as is used with **Privileged Identity Management** (**PIM**), where having rights doesn't necessarily mean that we can use them all the time; we have to activate/request for them to be used for a period of time.

> **Important note**
>
> JIT access for Azure Virtual Machines supports only VMs deployed through ARM (Azure Resource Manager). It's not available for non-Azure VMs or Azure VMs deployed through **Azure Service Management** (**ASR**).

JIT can be configured from the Azure Security Center blade, or from the Azure VM blade. Configuring JIT for an Azure VM requires a few parameters to be defined, such as which ports we want to use, whether we want to allow access from a specific IP address or range in the **Classless Inter-Domain Routing** (**CIDR**) format, and the maximum period of time access will be available.

An example of configuring JIT is shown in the following screenshot:

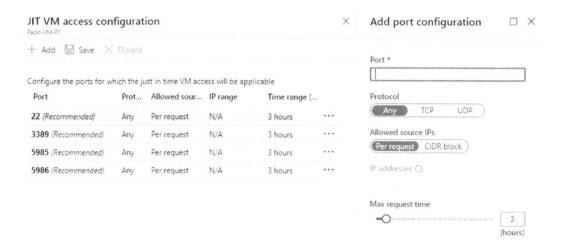

Figure. 7.15 – Configuring JIT access

By default, we have the most common management ports available. We can edit rules for these ports, delete rules, or add custom rules. Besides ports, we can change protocols, the allowed source, and the maximum request time (that can be between 1 and 24 hours).

Once JIT is configured, access needs to be requested each time we want to access the VM. This, again, can be done from the Azure Security Center blade or the Azure VM blade. While we are requesting, we can ask for a specific (or more than one) port to be opened, state whether we want to enable access from our current IP address or from an IP range, and finally, we need to define the time range. The time range depends on the configuration. By default, the time range is from 1 to 3 hours but can be configured for up to 24 hours.

Requesting JIT access is shown in the following screenshot:

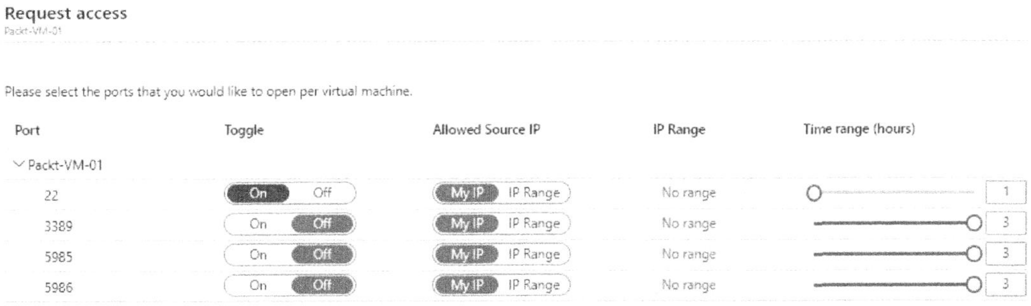

Figure. 7.16 – Requesting JIT access

JIT uses **Network Security Groups** (**NSGs**) to control traffic that is allowed or blocked. When JIT is configured for an Azure VM, NSG rules are created to block access over configured ports. Ports that are not configured for JIT should be automatically blocked unless configured otherwise. When JIT access is requested, another NSG is temporarily created that will allow access on the requested port. The new NSG rule will have a higher priority and override the block rule to enable access. Once the requested time period expires, the allow rule will be deleted, and access will be blocked again.

> **Important note**
> If JIT is in use, no NSG rules for management ports should be created manually. Azure Security Center should control these ports at all times. If we create rules manually, we may override JIT rules, or we may create a rule that will allow one of the management ports at all times and use JIT for the rest of the management ports. Both situations make JIT pointless.

Advanced network hardening analyzes our traffic communication patterns. Analysis is performed to determine whether NSG rules are overly permissive and create a threat in the form of an increased attack surface. Three potential threats are tracked: a malicious insider, data spillage, and data exfiltration. Azure Security Center reports all threats and assesses the current rules to determine whether changes to NSG rules are required and offers recommendations that will increase security.

File Integrity Monitoring is used to validate files and registries of the operating system and application software. It tracks changes and compares the current checksum of the file with the last scan of the same file to see whether they are different. Information can be used to determine whether changes are valid or the result of a malicious modification.

Threat protection

Threat protection provides information and reports on detected threats. It's very useful to have information on what is happening with our resources and whether anyone is trying anything against us.

> **Important note**
>
> No action will be performed by threat protection automatically; this section only provides information. To act on detected threats, we need to set up workflow automation.

Information provided in the threat protection section can be eye-opening. You might not even be the intended target but still get hacked as a victim of opportunity or due to a moment of carelessness.

To provide an example, we created an experiment where we deployed five Azure Virtual Machines and left the RDP port accessible over a private IP address. These were five blank VMs with no data and nothing special about them. What happens is that 'bad guys' scan public IP addresses in the hope of detecting open ports. After something like that is detected, a 'brute-force' attack will begin. Brute-force attacks use a combination of most common usernames and passwords to try to connect. These five Azure VMs, running for a single month, got hit approximately 20,000 times each.

All these attacks can be tracked and seen in Azure Security Center, in the threat protection section. An example of a report is shown in the following screenshot:

DESCRIPTION	Failed brute force attacks were detected from the following attackers: ['IP Address: 166.62.42.238']. Attackers were trying to access the host with the following user names: ['unknown user','sniffery','root'...'beverly'...'jenner'...'facade','www','dev'].
ACTIVITY TIME	Wednesday, December 25, 2019, 2:05:31 PM
SEVERITY	⚠ Medium
STATE	Active
ATTACKED RESOURCE	Linux-VM-01
SUBSCRIPTION	Microsoft Azure Sponsorship
DETECTED BY	▦ Microsoft
ACTION TAKEN	Detected
ENVIRONMENT	Azure
RESOURCE TYPE	🖥 Virtual Machine
NUMBER OF FAILED AUTHENTICATION ATTEMPTS TO HOST	146
WAS SSH SESSION INITIATED	No
REPORTS	Report: Brute Force

Figure. 7.17 – Bruce-force attack detected

In these reports, we can find information on which usernames were used in an attack, where the attack originated from, and how many times authentication was attempted. We can also see more information on the attack origin and the location from where the attack originated, as shown in the following screenshot:

⋀ Geo and Threat Intelligence Information

IP 61.189.59.250

Geo Information

IP ADDRESS	61.189.59.250
CITY	Yuhong Qu
COUNTRY CODE	CN
COUNTRY NAME	China
STATE	Liaoning
ASN	4837
LATITUDE	41.79073
LONGITUDE	123.2237

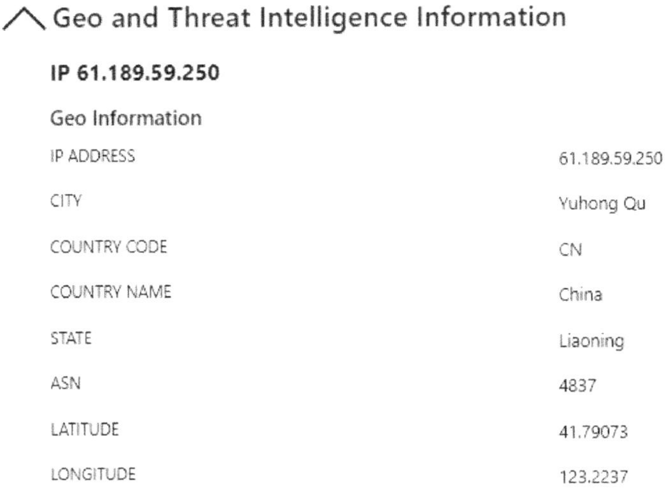

Figure. 7.18 – Bruce-force attack origin

Summary

Azure Security Center helps us to keep our cloud environment safe in various ways, from offering recommendations on what needs to be improved to detecting threats as they happen, to response automation to act on possible threats. With different settings and policies, we can define our focus, track the health of our resources, and create a more secure infrastructure.

In this chapter, we discussed how important Azure Security Center as a **Cloud Security Posture Management (CSPM)** and **Cloud Workload Protection Platform (CWPP)** tool is. The next chapter will focus on Azure Sentinel, which is Microsoft's cloud-based SIEM/SOAR solution.

Questions

1. Azure Security Center stores data in?

    A. Azure Storage

    B. Azure SQL Database

    C. Log Analytics workspace

2. Azure Security Center has which of the following pricing tiers?

    A. Free

    B. Standard

    C. Premium

    D. All of the above

    E. Only 1 and 2

    F. Only 2 and 3

3. Information on how to increase Azure security on our resources is provided in the form of?

    A. Fixes

    B. Recommendations

    C. Suggestions

4. We can automate responses to Azure Security Center alerts with?

   A. Log Analytics

   B. Logic Apps

   C. PowerShell

5. Which file type cannot be controlled with Adaptive Application Control?

   A. EXE

   B. JAR

   C. MSI

6. When JIT is enabled on an Azure VM, the user?

   A. Has the same access

   B. Has less access

   C. Has more access

   D. Has to request access

7. With **Advanced Threat Protection** (**ATP**), what happens when an attack occurs?

   A. It will be automatically blocked.

   B. The user has to create a response to the attack.

   C. Some attacks are blocked automatically, and the user has to create a custom response for unsupported attacks.

8
Azure Sentinel

Security Information and Event Management (**SIEM**) combines two solutions that were previously separate, **Security Information Management** (**SIM**) and **Security Event Management** (**SEM**).

We have already mentioned that large organizations rely on SIEM solutions. And Microsoft's SIEM solution for the cloud is Microsoft Azure Sentinel. But let's first take a step back and discuss what SIEM is and what functionalities it should have.

We will be covering the following topics in this chapter:

- Introduction to SIEM
- What is Azure Sentinel?
- Creating workbooks
- Using threat hunting and notebooks

Introduction to SIEM

Many security compliance standards require long-term storage, where security-related logs should be kept for long periods of time. This varies from one compliance standard to another and can be any period of time from 1 to 10 years. This is where SIM comes into the picture: long-term storage where all security-related logs are stored for analysis and reports.

When we speak of SEM, we tend to be talking about live data streaming rather than long-term event tracking. SEM's focus is on real-time monitoring; it aims to correlate events using notifications and dashboards. When we combine these two, we have SIEM, which tries to live stream all security-related logs and keep them for the long term. With this approach, we have a real-time monitoring and reporting tool in one solution.

When discussing the functionalities required, we have a few checkboxes that SIEM must tick:

- **Data aggregation**: Logs across different systems kept in a single place. This can include network, application, server, and database logs, to name a few.

- **Dashboards**: All aggregated data can be used to create charts. These charts can help us to visually detect patterns or anomalies.

- **Alerts**: Aggregated data is analyzed automatically, and any detected anomaly becomes an alert. Alerts are then sent to individuals or teams that must be aware or act.

- **Correlation**: One of SIEM's responsibilities is to provide a meaningful connection between common attributes and events. This is also where data aggregation comes in, because it helps to identify connected events across different log types. A single line in a database log may not mean much, but if it's combined with logs from the network and the application, it can help us prevent a disaster.

- **Retention**: As mentioned, one of the compliance requirements is to keep data for extended periods of time. But this also helps us to establish patterns over long periods of time and detect anomalies more easily.

- **Forensic analysis**: Once we are aware of a security issue, SIEM is used to analyze events and detect how and why the issue happened. This helps us to neutralize damage and prevent the issue from repeating.

To summarize, SIEM should have the ability to receive different data types in real time, provide meaning to received data, and store it for a long period of time. Received data is then analyzed to find patterns, detect anomalies, and help us prevent or stop security issues.

So, let's see how Azure Sentinel addresses these requirements.

Getting started with Azure Sentinel

Azure Sentinel is Microsoft's SIEM solution in the cloud. As cloud computing continues to revolutionize how we do IT, SIEM must evolve to address the new challenges that the changes to IT create. Azure Sentinel is a scalable cloud solution that offers intelligent security and threat analytics. On top of that, Azure Sentinel provides threat visibility and alerting, along with proactive threat hunting and responses.

So, if we look carefully, all the checkboxes for SIEM are ticked.

The pricing model for Azure Sentinel comes with two options:

- **Pay-As-You-Go**: In Pay-As-You-Go, billing is done per GB of data ingested to Azure Sentinel.

> **Important Note**
> At the time of writing, the price in the Pay-As-You-Go model was $2.60 per ingested GB.

- **Capacity reservation**: Capacity reservation offers different tiers with varying amounts of data reserved. Reservation creates a commitment and billing is done per tier, even if we don't use the reserved capacity. However, reservation provides a discount on ingested data and is a good option for organizations that expect large amounts of data.

The following diagram shows the capacity reservation prices for Azure Sentinel at the time of writing:

CAPACITY	PRICE
100 GB per day	$130 per day
200 GB per day	$234 per day
300 GB per day	$338 per day
400 GB per day	$433.33 per day
500 GB per day	$520 per day
More than 500 GB per day	$520 per day + $104 per day (for each 100 GB increment after 500 GB in daily capacity)

Figure 8.1 – Azure Sentinel pricing

If ingested data exceeds the reservation limit, further billing is done based on the Pay-As-You-Go model. For example, if we have a reserved capacity of 100 GB and we ingest 112 GB, we will pay the tier price for the reserved capacity up to 100 GB and will also pay for the additional 12 GB for the data that exceeds the reservation.

When enabling Azure Sentinel, we need to define the Log Analytics workspace that will be used for storing data. We can either create a new Log Analytics workspace or use an existing one.

Azure Sentinel uses Log Analytics for storing data. The price for Azure Sentinel does not include charges for Log Analytics.

> **Important Note**
>
> An additional charge for Log Analytics will be incurred for ingested data. Information about pricing can be found at `https://azure.microsoft.com/en-us/pricing/details/monitor/`.

In the following screenshot, we can see all the pricing options for Azure Sentinel at the time of writing:

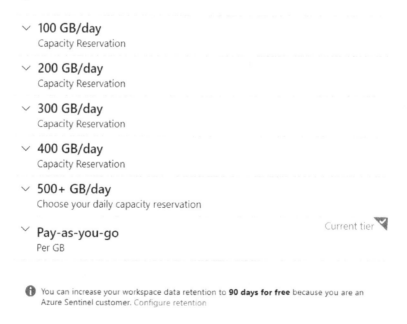

Figure 8.2 – Changing the Azure Sentinel pricing tier

Now, let's see how Azure Sentinel does everything that SIEM should be able to do. We will analyze all the requirements one by one and see how they are satisfied by Azure Sentinel.

Let's start with data connectors and retention configuring data connectors and retention

One of SIEM's requirements is data aggregation. However, data aggregation doesn't just mean collecting data, but also the ability to collect data from multiple sources. Azure Sentinel does this really well and has many integrated connectors. At this time (and more connectors are introduced constantly), there are 32 connectors available. Most of the connectors are for different Microsoft sources, such as Azure Active Directory, Azure Active Directory Identity Protection, Azure Security Center, Microsoft Cloud App Security or Office365, to name but a few. But there are also connectors for data sources outside the Microsoft ecosystem, such as Amazon Web Services, Barracuda Firewalls, Cisco, Citrix, and Palo Alto Networks.

> **Important Note**
>
> For more information on connectors, you can refer to the following link:
> `https://docs.microsoft.com/en-us/azure/sentinel/`
> `connect-data-sources`

The data connectors page is shown in the following screenshot:

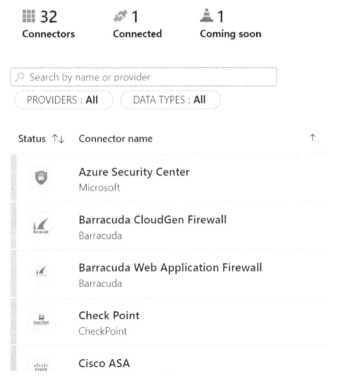

Figure 8.3 – Azure Sentinel data connectors

All data connectors include step-by-step instructions explaining how to configure data sources to send data. It's important to mention that all the data is stored in Log Analytics. Instructions vary from data source to data source. Most Microsoft data sources can be added by just enabling a connection from one service to another. Other data sources require the installation of an agent or editing of the endpoint's configuration.

There are many default connectors in Azure Sentinel. Beside the obvious Microsoft connectors with services in Azure and Office365, we have many connectors for on-premises services as well. But it doesn't stop there, and many other connectors are available, such as Amazon Web Services, Barracuda, Cisco, Palo Alto, F5, and Symantec.

Once the data is imported into Log Analytics and is ready to be used in Azure Sentinel, that is when the real work starts.

Working with Azure Sentinel Dashboards

After the data is gathered, the next step is to display data using various dashboards. Dashboards visually present data using **Key Performance Indicators (KPIs)**, metrics, and key data points in order to monitor security events. Presenting data visually helps set up baseline patterns and detect anomalies.

The following screenshot shows events and alerts over time:

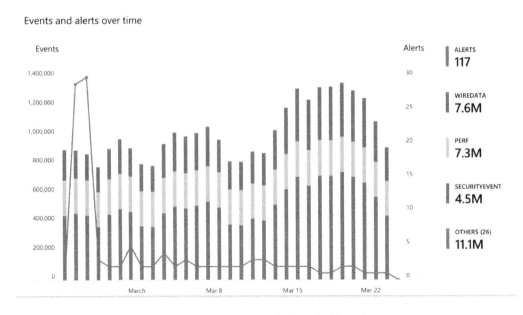

Figure 8.4 – Events and alerts dashboard

In this screenshot, we can see how the baseline is established. There is a similar number of events over time. Any sudden increase or decrease would be an anomaly that we would need to investigate.

The events over time dashboard uses metrics to display data. But we can also use KPIs to create different types of dashboard. The following diagram shows anomalies in the data source:

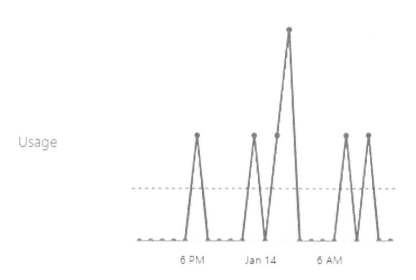

Figure 8.5 – Anomalies dashboard

These two examples represent default dashboards that are available when Azure Sentinel is enabled. We can also create custom dashboards, based on the requirements and the KPIs defined.

However, this is only the first step in detecting something that's out of the ordinary. We need additional steps to automate the process.

Setting up rules and alerts

The only problem with dashboards is that they are useful if someone is watching them. Data is displayed visually, and we can detect issues only if we are monitoring dashboards at all times. But what happens when no one is watching? For these situations, we define rules and alerts.

Using rules, we can define a baseline and send notifications (or even automate responses) when any type of anomaly appears. In Azure Sentinel, we can create custom rules on the **Analytics** blade, with two types of rules available:

- The first type of rule is the **Microsoft incident creation rule**, where we can select from a list of predefined analytic rules. The rules here are **Microsoft Cloud App Security**, **Azure Security Center**, **Azure Advanced Threat protection**, **Azure Active Directory Identity Protection**, and **Microsoft Defender Advanced Threat Protection**. The only other option is to select the severity of the incident that will be tracked.

- The second type of rule is **Scheduled query rule**. We have more options here, and we can define rules that track basically anything. The only limitation we have here is our data. The more data we have, the more things we can track. Using **Kusto Query Language**, we can create custom rules and check for any type of information as long as the data is already in the Log Analytics workspace.

To create a custom query rule, the following steps are required:

1. We need to define a name, select the tactics, and set the severity we want to detect. There are several tactics options we can choose from: Initial Access, Execution, Persistence, Privileged Escalation, Defense Evasion, Credential Access, Discovery, Lateral Movement, Collection, Exfiltration, Command and Control, and Impact.

   Optionally, we can add a description. Adding a description is recommended because it can help us track down rules and detect their purpose. An example is shown in the following screenshot:

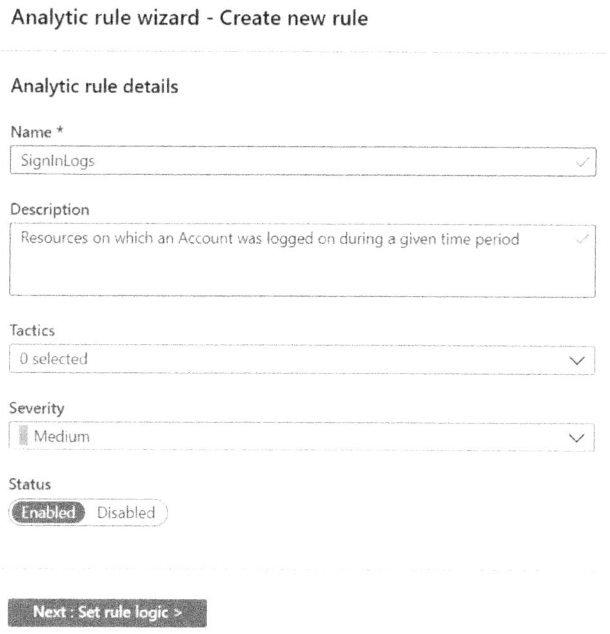

Analytic rule wizard - Create new rule

Analytic rule details

Name *

SignInLogs

Description

Resources on which an Account was logged on during a given time period

Tactics

0 selected

Severity

Medium

Status

Enabled Disabled

Next : Set rule logic >

Figure 8.6 – Creating a new analytics rule

Next, we need to set the rule's logic. In this part, we need to set up the rule query using Kusto Query Language. The query will be executed against data in Log Analytics in order to detect any events that represent a threat or an issue. The query needs to be correct because the syntax will be checked. A failed syntax check will result in the query failing to proceed. An example of a query in a custom rule is shown in the following screenshot:

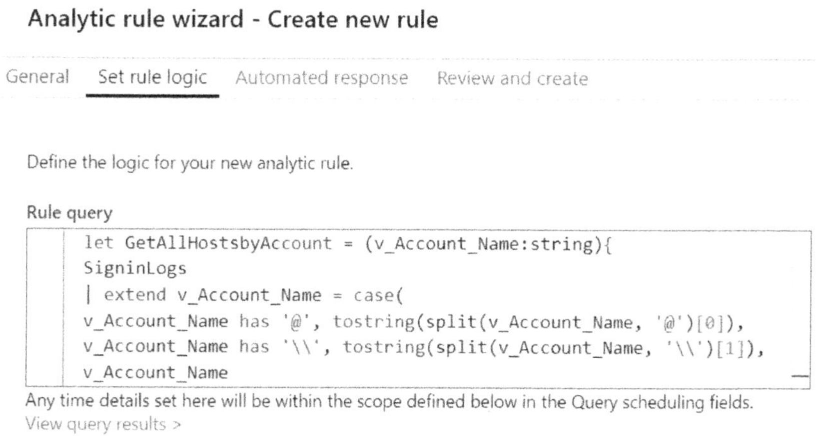

Analytic rule wizard - Create new rule

General   Set rule logic   Automated response   Review and create

Define the logic for your new analytic rule.

Rule query

```
let GetAllHostsbyAccount = (v_Account_Name:string){
SigninLogs
| extend v_Account_Name = case(
v_Account_Name has '@', tostring(split(v_Account_Name, '@')[0]),
v_Account_Name has '\\', tostring(split(v_Account_Name, '\\')[1]),
v_Account_Name
```

Any time details set here will be within the scope defined below in the Query scheduling fields.
View query results >

Figure 8.7 – Defining an analytic rule query

The query used in this example is tracking resources on the account that were logged in the last 24 hours, which you can see here:

```
let GetAllHostsbyAccount = (v_Account_Name:string){
  SigninLogs
  | extend v_Account_Name = case(
  v_Account_Name has '@', tostring(split(v_Account_Name,
'@')[0]),
  v_Account_Name has '\\', tostring(split(v_Account_Name,
'\\')[1]),
  v_Account_Name
  )
  | where UserPrincipalName contains v_Account_Name
  | extend RemoteHost =
tolower(tostring(parsejson(DeviceDetail.
['displayName'])))
  | extend OS = DeviceDetail.operatingSystem, Browser =
DeviceDetail.browser
  | extend StatusCode = tostring(Status.errorCode),
StatusDetails = tostring(Status.additionalDetails)
  | extend State = tostring(LocationDetails.state), City
= tostring(LocationDetails.city)
  | extend info = pack('UserDisplayName',
UserDisplayName, 'UserPrincipalName', UserPrincipalName,
'AppDisplayName', AppDisplayName, 'ClientAppUsed',
ClientAppUsed, 'Browser', tostring(Browser), 'IPAddress',
IPAddress, 'ResultType', ResultType, 'ResultDescription',
ResultDescription, 'Location', Location, 'State', State,
'City', City, 'StatusCode', StatusCode, 'StatusDetails',
StatusDetails)
  | summarize min(TimeGenerated), max(TimeGenerated),
Host_Aux_info = makeset(info) by RemoteHost ,
tostring(OS)
  | project min_TimeGenerated, max_TimeGenerated,
RemoteHost, OS, Host_Aux_info
  | top 10 by min_TimeGenerated desc nulls last
  | project-rename Host_UnstructuredName=RemoteHost,
Host_OSVersion=OS
```

```
    };
    // change <Name> value below
    GetAllHostsbyAccount('<Name>')
```

2. Once the query is defined, we need to create the schedule. The schedule defines how often the query is executed and the data that it's executed against. We also define the threshold for when an event becomes an alert. For example, a failed login attempt is just an event. But if this event repeats over time, then it becomes an alert.

    The following screenshot shows an example of a schedule and a threshold:

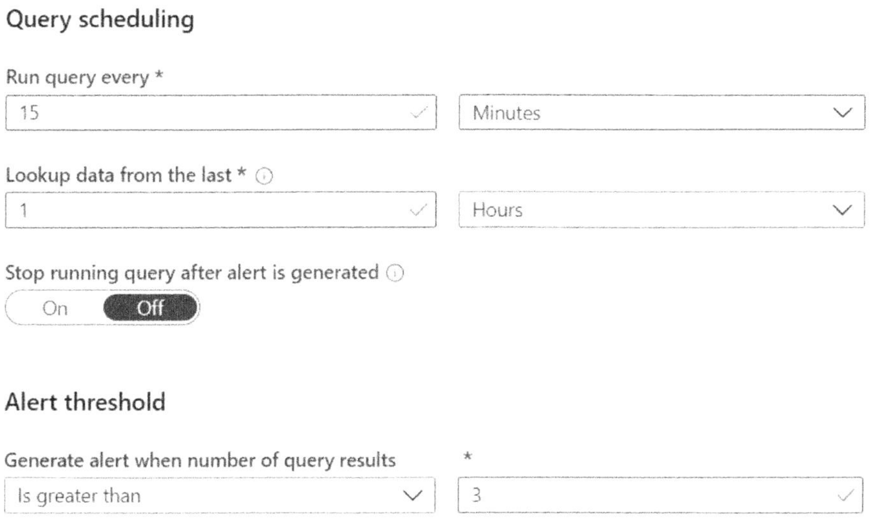

    ### Query scheduling

    Run query every *

15		Minutes	∨

    Lookup data from the last * ⓘ

1		Hours	∨

    Stop running query after alert is generated ⓘ

    (On **Off**)

    ### Alert threshold

    Generate alert when number of query results   *

Is greater than	∨	3	

    Figure 8.8 – Analytic rule scheduling

3. In the last step, we can define what will happen when the alert is triggered. Similar to workflow automation in Azure Security Center (in *Chapter 7*, *Azure Security Center*), logic apps are used to create automated responses. These responses can be either notifications (to users or groups of users) or automated responses that will react to stop or prevent the threat.

An example of creating a new logic app is shown in the following screenshot:

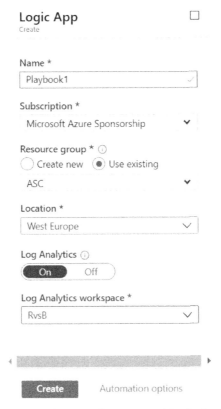

Figure 8.9 – Automated response with a logic app

But in modern cybersecurity, this may not be enough. We need to respond in a matter of seconds and we need the ability to track specific events related to security.

Creating workbooks

In Azure Sentinel, we can use workbooks to define what we want to monitor and how we do it. Similar to alert rules, we have the option to use predefined templates or to create custom alerts. In contrast with alert rules, with workbooks, we create dashboards in order to monitor data in real time.

At this moment, there are 39 templates available, and this list is very similar to the list of data connectors. Basically, there is at least one workbook template for each data connector. We can choose any template for the list displayed in the following screenshot:

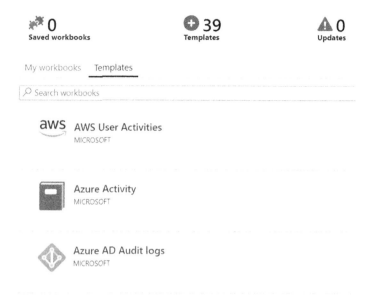

Figure 8.10 – Azure Sentinel workbook templates

Each template will enable an additional dashboard that is customized to monitor a certain data source. In the following screenshot, we can see the dashboard for Azure activities:

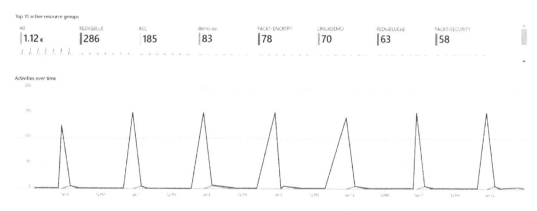

Figure 8.11 – Azure Activity template

The story doesn't end here. With Azure Sentinel, we can leverage machine learning and embed intelligence in our security layer.

Using threat hunting and notebooks

In Azure Sentinel, with dashboards and alerts, we can look for anomalies and issues, but in modern IT we need more. Cyber threats are becoming more and more sophisticated. Traditional methods of detecting issues and threats are not enough. By the time we detect issues, it may already be too late. We need to be proactive and look for possible issues and stop threats before they occur.

For threat hunting, there is a separate section in Azure Sentinel. It allows us to create custom queries, but also offers an extensive list of pre-created queries to help us start. Some of the queries for proactive threat hunting are high reverse DNS count, domains linked with the WannaCry ransomware, failed login attempts, hosts with new logins, and unusual logins, to name a few. A list of some of the available queries is shown in the following screenshot:

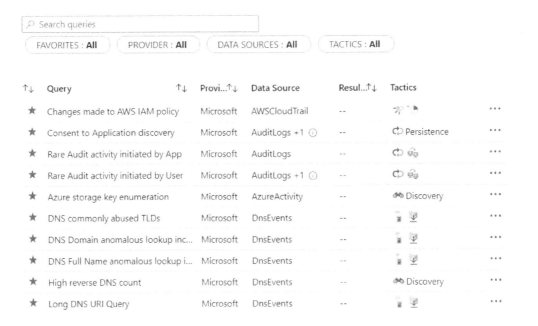

Figure 8.12 – Queries for threat hunting

We can also switch view to live stream and use it to watch for certain events in real time. Live stream offers a graphical view of our hunting queries to help us monitor threats visually.

Another option in the hunting section is bookmarks. When exploring data and looking for threats, we may encounter events that we are not sure about. Some events may look innocent, but, in combination with other events, may prove very dangerous. Bookmarks allow us to save the results of some queries in order to revisit them later. We may want to check the same thing in the next few days and compare results, or maybe check some other logs that may give us more information.

Proactive hunting does not stop there. There is another section in Azure Sentinel, called notebooks. Azure Sentinel is a data store that uses powerful queries and scaling to analyze data in massive volumes. Notebooks goes one step further, and with common APIs, allows the use of Jupyter Notebooks and Python. These tools extend what we can do with data stored in Azure Sentinel, allowing us to use a huge collection of libraries for machine learning, visualization, and complex analysis.

Again, we have some notebooks already available that we can start using right away. The list of available queries is shown in the following screenshot:

Notebook name	↑	Status
Entity Explorer - Account Microsoft		t version update: 10/30/19, 01:00 AM Hunting
Entity Explorer - Domain and URL Microsoft		t version update: 10/21/19, 02:00 AM Hunting
Entity Explorer - IP Address Microsoft		t version update: 10/29/19, 01:00 AM Hunting
Entity Explorer - Linux Host Microsoft		t version update: 10/17/19, 02:00 AM Hunting
Entity Explorer - Windows Host Microsoft		t version update: 10/18/19, 02:00 AM Hunting
Guided Investigation - Anomaly Lookup Microsoft		t version update: 07/31/19, 02:00 AM Investigation
Guided Investigation - Process Alerts Microsoft		t version update: 04/23/19, 02:00 AM Investigation

Figure 8.13 – Azure Sentinel notebooks

Azure Sentinel isn't just a tool with a limited number of options; it's also very customizable. There are many ways to adjust Azure Sentinel to your specific needs and requirements. There are many external resources that can be used or further adjusted.

Using community resources

The power of Azure Sentinel is extended by its community. There is a Git repository at `https://github.com/Azure/Azure-Sentinel`. Here, we can find many additional resources that we can use. Resources developed by the community offer new dashboards, hunting queries, exploration queries, playbooks for automated responses, and much, much more.

The community repository is a very useful collection of resources that we can use to extend Azure Sentinel with additional capabilities and increase security even further.

Summary

Azure Sentinel satisfies all the requirements for SIEM. Not only that, it also brings additional tools to the table in the form of proactive threat hunting and using machine learning and predictive algorithms. With all the other resources we have covered, most aspects of modern security have been covered, from identity and governance over network and data protection, to monitoring health, detecting issues, and preventing threats.

But security does not end here. Almost every resource in Azure has some security options enabled. These options can help us go even further and improve security. With all the cybersecurity threats around today, we need to take every precaution available.

In the final chapter, we are going to discuss security best practices and how to use every security option to our advantage.

Questions

1. Azure Sentinel is…

    A. Security Event Management (SEM)

    B. Security Information Management (SIM)

    C. Security Information Event Management (SIEM)

2. Azure Sentinel stores data in…

    A. Azure Storage

    B. Azure SQL Database

    C. A Log Analytics workspace

3. Which data connectors are supported in Azure Sentinel?

   A. Microsoft data connectors

   B. Cloud data connectors

   C. A variety of data connectors from different vendors

4. Which query language is used in Azure Sentinel?

   A. SQL

   B. GraphQL

   C. Kusto

5. Dashboards in Azure Sentinel are used for...

   A. Visual detection of issues

   B. Constant monitoring

   C. Threat prevention

6. Rules and alerts in Azure Sentinel are used for...

   A. Visual detection of issues

   B. Constant monitoring

   C. Threat prevention

7. Threat hunting is performed by....

   A. Monitoring dashboards

   B. Using Kusto queries

   C. Analyzing data with Jupyter Notebook

9
Security Best Practices

In this book, we have already covered the most important topics regarding Azure security, from governance and monitoring to identity, network, and data protection, to specific tools such as Azure Security Center and Azure Sentinel. In this final chapter, you will find some tips and tricks the authors are using regularly in their projects.

The topics we will cover in the following sections include the following:

- Log Analytics design considerations
- Understanding Azure SQL Database security features
- Security in Azure App Service

Log Analytics design considerations

You've already learned that Azure Security Center and Azure Sentinel rely heavily on Azure Log Analytics. But there are some important considerations to make before you start your security monitoring journey in the cloud.

The two most important paradigms in this context are these:

- Using as few Log Analytics workspaces as possible
- Using regional workspaces to avoid Azure bandwidth costs

From a technical point of view, it's the best idea to only use a single, central workspace so all the data resides in one place. Having a single workspace, you can easily, efficiently, and quickly correlate your data to get the respective insights. You also only need to take care of a single **role-based access control** (**RBAC**) model for this workspace. However, fine-grained RBAC models demand more effort.

From a monetary point of view, however, you should plan for regional workspaces instead of a central workspace if you are using Azure resources in different Azure regions. For on-premises servers, it does not make a big difference what layout you are planning for because all **incoming network traffic** (**ingress**) to an Azure region is free. The Microsoft Monitoring Agent will send data to Azure, but there is no regular data transfer from Azure to your on-premises servers. The problem is that you must pay for **outgoing traffic** (**egress**) out of an Azure region. Now, if you use a single, central Log Analytics workspace and have Azure **Virtual Machines** (**VMs**) deployed in different Azure regions, outgoing data transfers from these VMs to your workspace would generate traffic costs.

In order to bring both paradigms together, the idea is to create one single workspace in every Azure region you are using, not only to avoid regular traffic costs but also to still stick to the idea of having as few workspaces as possible.

If you use several workspaces, you can no longer use auto-provisioning in Azure Security Center. Because of the automation process, you can only configure one workspace per subscription. Since an Azure subscription can contain resources from all, or at least several, Azure regions, depending on your policies, you need another way to automatically deploy the Microsoft Monitoring Agent to your Azure VM. This is where **Infrastructure as Code** (**IaC**) comes into play. With **Azure Resource Manager** (**ARM**) templates, Terraform, or PowerShell, you can deploy Azure VM and install the Log Analytics VM extension at the same time. The Log Analytics VM extension is deployed and managed through the ARM and fully supports CI/CD pipelines in your DevOps scenario. That said, when you use IaC deployments for your VM in your DevOps scenario, you can also update, manage, and configure the agent through your pipeline. If you then also have configured policies, blueprints, and all the other governance features you have learned about in *Chapter 2, Governance and Security*, you can easily adhere to your corporate security policy and leverage automation at the same time.

Next, we are going to look at other Azure services' security features and how they can help us increase security.

Understanding Azure SQL Database security features

Some security features related to Azure SQL Database were mentioned in *Chapter 6, Data Security*, where we discussed data security. But there are additional features we can use to increase security.

The first feature and line of defense when it comes to Azure SQL Database is a firewall. This built-in tool, by default, blocks access to the database from any IP address that is not preauthorized (whitelisted). It's important to mention that firewall settings are on the Azure SQL Server level and will be inherited to all databases on the server. If we need to allow access to one IP address to a single database, we may want to reconsider our resource strategy. Allowing an IP address to access a single database will enable access to all databases on the same server. Because of this, we need to consider putting only databases used by the same applications or the same group of users on a single server.

Allowing a new IP address to connect to Azure SQL Server can be done from the Azure SQL Server firewall settings. We have the option to add a single IP address (the start and end IP will be the same), or add a range of IP addresses (from the start IP to the end IP). If we want to allow our current IP address, there is a convenient **Add client IP** button. This will automatically detect the IP address we are coming from and add a new rule to allow that IP address. After any rule is added, we need to save changes in order for them to become effective.

An example of firewall settings is shown in the following figure:

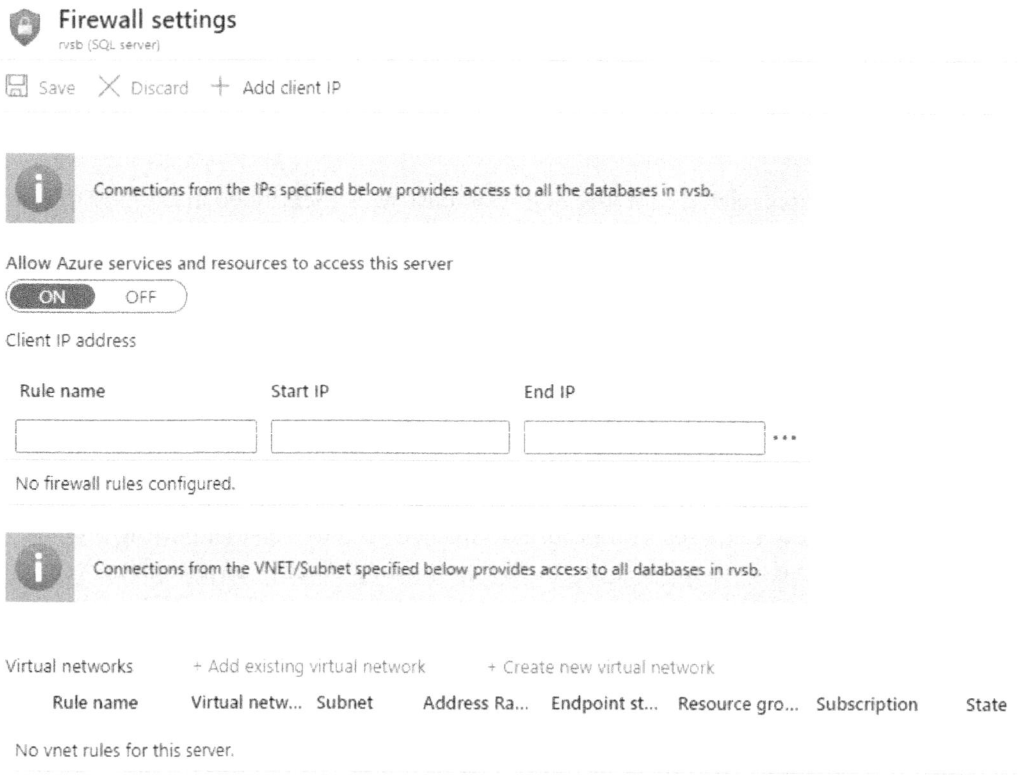

Firewall settings
rvsb (SQL server)

🖫 Save   ✕ Discard   + Add client IP

ℹ️ Connections from the IPs specified below provides access to all the databases in rvsb.

Allow Azure services and resources to access this server

(**ON** OFF)

Client IP address

Rule name	Start IP	End IP
		...

No firewall rules configured.

ℹ️ Connections from the VNET/Subnet specified below provides access to all databases in rvsb.

Virtual networks   + Add existing virtual network   + Create new virtual network

Rule name	Virtual netw...	Subnet	Address Ra...	Endpoint st...	Resource gro...	Subscription	State

No vnet rules for this server.

Figure 9.1 – Azure SQL Server firewall settings

Under **Firewall settings**, there are two additional options we can use:

- **Allow Azure services and resources to access this server**
- **Connections from the VNET/Subnet**

The option to allow Azure services sounds compelling, but we need to be very careful. At first look, this option looks helpful and most people will probably think they should allow Azure services to connect. It makes our life so much easier when we don't have to worry about how our web app connects to a database. But this option does not allow only your Azure service to connect, it allows any Azure service to connect. Allowing Azure services and resources to connect will only check if the connection is coming from an Azure data center, it will not limit connection to your subscription or tenant. Allowing this option will make Azure SQL Database more vulnerable, and I would recommend you keep this option off.

> **Important Note**
>
> **Allow Azure services and resources to access this server** is set to **OFF** by default, but it wasn't always the case. Previously, this setting was enabled by default. If you have Azure SQL Database already created, make sure this setting is disabled.

Connection from VNET/Subnet allows us to create VNET integration by allowing certain VNET (or limiting this only to subnets) to connect to Azure SQL Database. This approach is more secure as the database does not need to be exposed over the internet and all communication is done on a secure private network.

But Azure SQL Database is just one example of built-in security features on a service level. Almost every service has some service-specific security features. Azure App Service is another excellent example with many security options available, which we will be covering next.

Security in Azure App Service

Azure App Service is an HTTP-based service for hosting web applications and APIs, with support for multiple programming languages. It's also another great example of an Azure service with multiple security features built-in. We can control access, protocols, certificates, and many other things.

One of the early problems we need to solve for any application is authentication. App Service allows us to set up authentication based on a few different providers: **Azure Active Directory** (**Azure AD**), Microsoft (or Live) account, Facebook, Google, and Twitter. Naturally, the best integration method is using Azure AD, as it is native and also allows you further control through Azure AD tools and features.

In order to set up Azure AD authentication for App Service, we need to do the following:

1. In the **App Service Authentication** blade, we need to select **Azure Active Directory**, as in the following figure:

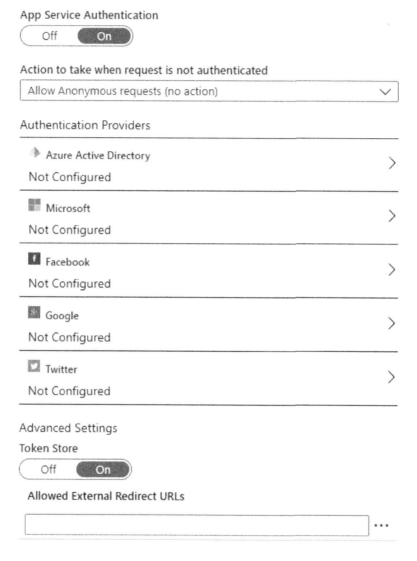

Figure 9.2 – Azure App Service authentication

2. We have two options in authentication settings. If we choose **Express**, this will create a service principal and all required permissions for us automatically. If we choose **Advanced** settings, we will need to provide a service principal and create permissions ourselves. The following figure shows an example of **Express** settings:

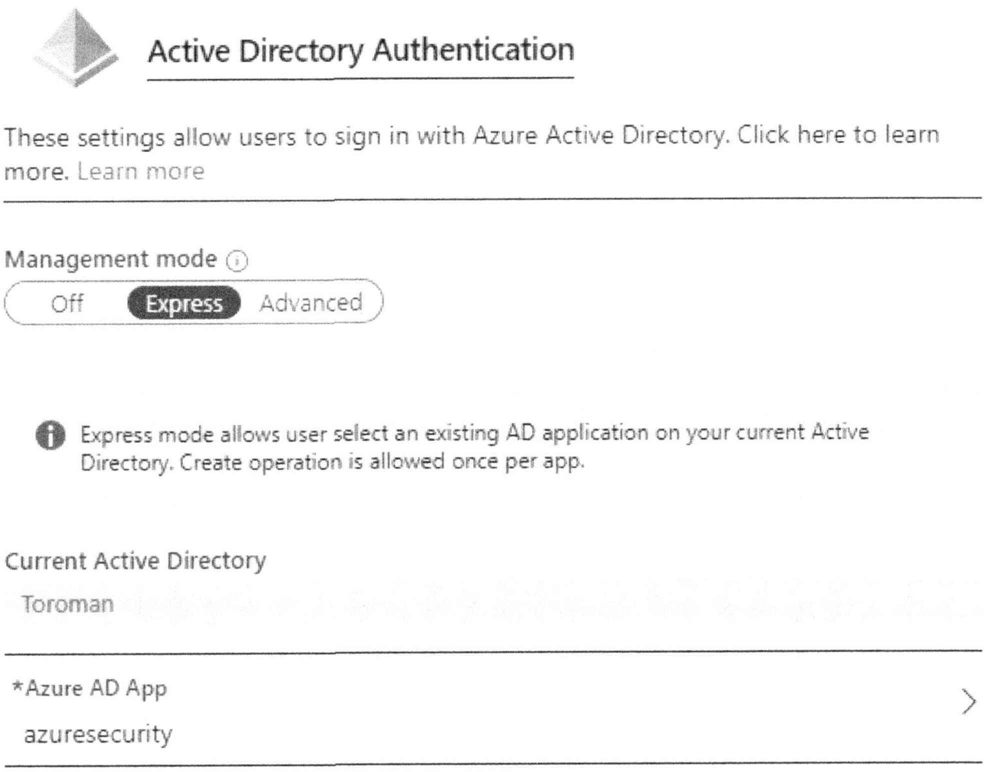

 Active Directory Authentication

These settings allow users to sign in with Azure Active Directory. Click here to learn more. Learn more

Management mode ⓘ

(Off **Express** Advanced)

ⓘ Express mode allows user select an existing AD application on your current Active Directory. Create operation is allowed once per app.

Current Active Directory

Toroman

*Azure AD App   ⟩

azuresecurity

Figure 9.3 – App Service Azure AD authentication

3. After everything is configured, we need to ensure that the user is required to log in with **Azure Active Directory** in order to access the application, as in the following figure:

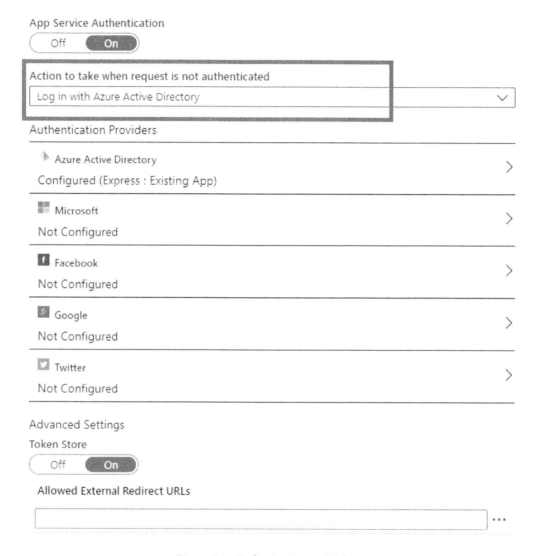

Figure 9.4 – Enforcing Azure AD login

4. When accessing the application, the user will be prompted to **Sign in** with their Azure AD account in order to proceed, as in the following figure:

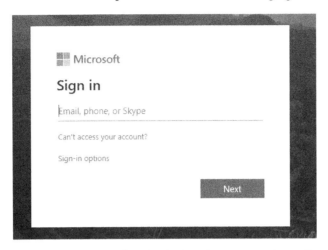

Figure 9.5 – User is required to sign in in order to access the application

Another set of security features in Azure App Service is **Protocol Settings**. Here, we can force the application to use only HTTPS, control the minimal TLS version, or if an incoming client certificate is required. We can also configure **TLS/SSL bindings** to specify the certificate that will be used when responding to a request to a specific hostname. Both public and private certificates can be used:

Protocol Settings

Protocol settings are global and apply to all bindings defined by your app.

ⓘ Some custom hostnames for your app are missing SSL bindings. When HTTPS Only is enabled clients accessing your app on those custom hostnames will see security warnings. To fix this add the missing SSL bindings or remove the custom hostnames.

HTTPS Only: ⓘ   Off   **On**

Minimum TLS Version ⓘ   1.0   1.1   **1.2**

Incoming client certificates ⓘ   **Off**   On

TLS/SSL bindings

Bindings let you specify which certificate to use when responding to requests to a specific hostname over HTTPS. TLS/SSL Binding requires valid private certificate (.pfx) issued for the specific hostname. Learn more

+ Add TLS/SSL Binding

Host name	Private Certificate Thumbprint	TLS/SSL Type

No TLS/SSL bindings configured for the app.

Figure 9.6 – App Service protocol settings

Private certificates can be imported from App Service (to a specific web app), uploaded, imported from Azure Key Vault, or we can create a new **App Service Managed Certificate**.

> **Note**
>
> **App Service Managed Certificate** is available to all web apps on App Service, not just on the web app where it's created.

In the following figure, we can see the **Private Key Certificate** settings:

Figure 9.7 – App Service private key certificate

Public Key Certificate requires a certificate issued by a recognized **Certificate Authority** (**CA**). This certificate is usually used by publicly accessible web applications, and serves as proof that the website is trustworthy:

Figure 9.8 – Public key certificate

Under networking settings in App Service, we have multiple options. Most of the options are related to secure connections and the integration of a web app with private networks. This was already mentioned in *Chapter 4, Azure Network Security*, when we discussed network security. We can achieve this with both VNET integration and hybrid connections. Also, this section includes options to enable services such as Azure Front Door (as the web application firewall for globally distributed applications) and **Content Delivery Network (CDN)**. The last option under network settings is access restrictions. All network settings associated with Azure App Service are shown in the following figure:

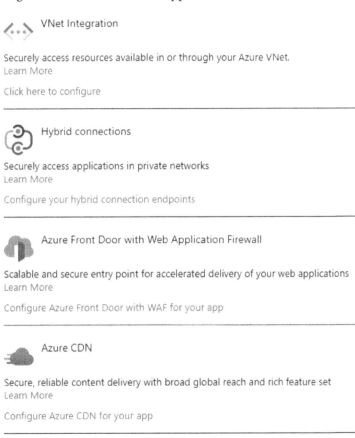

Figure 9.9 – Azure App Service network settings

Access Restrictions is a very useful feature in **Azure App Service** settings. Using **Access Restrictions**, we can block access from specific IP addresses or allow access only from whitelisted IP addresses. Essentially, **Access Restrictions** works very similarly to **Network Security Groups** (**NSGs**), by creating rules and assigning priority to them. However, **Access Restrictions** focuses on public access where NSGs control broader networks with both public and private network rules. In the following figure, we can see an example of creating a block rule:

Figure 9.10 – App Service Access restriction

To create a block rule, we need to provide the following information:

- **Name**
- **Action** (allow or deny access)
- **Priority**
- **Description**
- **Type** (IPv4 or IPv6)
- **IP Address Block**

In the preceding example, a rule is created to block access from IP address block
208.130.0.0/16. If anyone tries to access the application from any IP address in the
specified IP address range, the request will be blocked and the user will be prevented from
reaching the web app.

As we are able to use priorities, we can also approach things differently, and allow access
only from whitelisted IP addresses. In this case, we would create a block rule that would
prevent anyone from accessing the application and assign **Priority** 200. Another rule
would be created to allow access from a specific IP address range with **Priority** 100 (this
can be any value under 200). Allowing a rule for specified IP addresses would override
the rule to block, because of its higher priority. But it would still prevent anyone else from
accessing the application.

Another challenge we face with the cloud is secrets management. We need to be careful
how secrets, connections strings, and other sensitive information are used and make
sure that none of these are exposed. As in many cases we have already discussed in this
book, Azure Key Vault comes to the rescue. Similar to passing secrets when using IaC (as
discussed in *Chapter 5, Azure Key Vault*), or managing keys and certificates (discussed in
Chapter 6, Data Security), Azure Key Vault can be used to secure any sensitive information
needed by Azure App Service. Instead of storing sensitive information in web config files
or in App Service Configuration (where information is hidden, but visible if the user
has enough permissions), we can use a managed identity that will allow access to Azure
Key Vault, where sensitive information is stored in a secure way. An example of identity
settings in App Service is shown in the following figure:

Figure 9.11 – Managed identity in Azure App Service

As we can see, there are two types of managed identity that we can set: **System assigned** and **User assigned**. **System assigned** will generate a managed identity and set up necessary options. In **User assigned**, we need to create a managed identity ourselves, and create any necessary permissions and settings. If we require using more than one managed identity for a service, we need to use a **User assigned** managed identity, because a service can have only one system-assigned managed identity.

A **System assigned** managed identity is tied to a resource life cycle, and once a resource is removed, the managed identity is removed as well. The managed identity is generated in order to be used for that service and is not used by any other service. This is not the case with a **User assigned** identity, as more resources can use the same managed identity.

Summary

At the very end of this book, we have covered all aspects of Microsoft Azure security. From the shared responsibility model to advanced security features, we have come to an end. It's important to remember that the cloud changes all the time, and more and more services are available that can help us to increase security.

Let's focus on the most important takeaways from this book:

- Keep your identity and secrets secure with all the means available.
- When it comes to access, take two approaches: **Just Enough Administration** (**JEA**) and **Just-in-Time Administration** (**JIT Administration**).
- Nothing should be exposed to public access if it's not necessary, especially management and security access.
- Data should be encrypted at all times.
- All communication and traffic should be encrypted (over HTTPS) and on a secure (private) network, if possible.
- Azure Security Center and Azure Sentinel can help you with analytics, detection, and recommendations to stay on top of cloud security and keep Azure resources safe.
- Besides services focused on security, all Azure services have security features of their own. Use these features to increase security.

Microsoft Azure changes all the times; new features are added, and existing features are updated almost daily. So, in the future, options might change, but these options are there to present an idea of how to approach cloud security. These seven key points are what we need to focus on; how we complete these tasks is insignificant.

Questions

1. What is Log Analytics best practice?

   A. Use a single workspace

   B. Use regional workspaces

   C. Use multiple workspaces for each region and each service

2. We can control access to Azure SQL Database with…

   A. An access list

   B. A firewall

   C. Conditional access

3. Which type of certificate is supported in Azure App Service?

   A. Private

   B. Public

   C. Wildcard

   D. All of the above

   E. Only 1 and 2

   F. Only 2 and 3

4. We can control access to Azure App Service with…

   A. Access restriction

   B. A firewall

   C. Conditional access

5. What is used to enable App Service communication with other Azure services?

   A. Service Principal

   B. Managed identity

   C. Azure Key Vault

6. Azure App Service supports authentication with…

    A. Azure Active Directory (Azure AD)

    B. Microsoft account

    C. Twitter

    D. All of the above

    E. Only 1 and 2

    F. Only 2 and 3

7. Security in Azure can be set up from…

    A. Azure Security Center

    B. Azure Sentinel

    C. Different services and features

    D. Azure AD

Further reading

- *Hands-On Cloud Administration in Azure* by Mustafa Toroman: `https://www.packtpub.com/virtualization-and-cloud/hands-cloud-administration-azure`.

- *Azure Administration Cookbook* by Kamil Mrzyglod: `https://www.packtpub.com/cloud-networking/azure-administration-cookbook`.

- *Active Directory Administration Cookbook* by Sander Berkouwer: `https://www.packtpub.com/virtualization-and-cloud/active-directory-administration-cookbook`.

- *Azure Networking Cookbook* by Mustafa Toroman: `https://www.packtpub.com/virtualization-and-cloud/azure-networking-cookbook`.

- *Hands-On Azure for Developers* by Kamil Mrzyglod: `https://www.packtpub.com/virtualization-and-cloud/hands-azure-developers`.

Assessments

Chapter 1: Azure Security Introduction

Here are some sample answers to the questions presented in this chapter:

1. Answer **C.** Responsibility is shared
2. Answer **B.** Cloud provider
3. Answer **B.** Cloud provider
4. Answer **C.** Depends on service model
5. Answer **A.** User
6. Answer **D.** Both, but Q10 is replacing DLA
7. Answer **C.** Customer is notified

Chapter 2: Governance and Security

Here are some sample answers to the questions presented in this chapter:

1. Answer **D.** All of the above
2. Answer **D.** Depends on deployment method
3. Answer **C.** Management locks
4. Answer **B.** Management group
5. Answer **B.** Subscription
6. Answer **C.** Both of the above
7. Answer **B.** Service to gather information

Chapter 3: Governance and Security

Here are some sample answers to the questions presented in this chapter:

1. Answer **A.** More exposed to attacks

2. Answer **C.** Password protection

3. Answer **C. Multi-Factor Authentication** (MFA)

4. Answer **A.** Yes

5. Answer **C.** Infected users

6. Answer **C.** To activate privileges

7. Answer **C.** Passwordless

Chapter 4: Azure Network Security

Here are some sample answers to the questions presented in this chapter:

1. Answer **B. Network Security Group** (NSG)

2. Answer **B.** Site-to-Site

3. Answer **C.** Both of the above

4. Answer **B.** Service endpoints

5. Answer **E.** 1 and 3 are correct

6. Answer **B. Web Application Firewall** (WAF)

7. Answer **C. Distributed Denial of Service** (DDoS)

Chapter 5: Azure Key Vault

Here are some sample answers to the questions presented in this chapter:

1. Answer **D.** All of the above

2. Answer **B.** Access policies

3. Answer **A.** Service Principal

4. Answer **A.** EnabledForDeployment

5. Answer **B.** EnabledForTemplateDeployment

6. Answer **C.** EnabledForDiskEncryption

7. Answer **C.** Reference Azure Key Vault

Chapter 6: Data Security

Here are some sample answers to the questions presented in this chapter:

1. Answer **B.** Enforce HTTPS
2. Answer **C.** Blob soft delete
3. Answer **A.** Yes
4. Answer **B.** No
5. Answer **B.** No
6. Answer **C.** Both of the above
7. Answer **C. Transparent Database Encryption (TDE)**

Chapter 7: Azure Security Center

Here are some sample answers to the questions presented in this chapter:

1. Answer **C.** Log Analytics workspace
2. Answer **E.** Only 1 and 2
3. Answer **B.** Recommendations
4. Answer **B.** Logic Apps
5. Answer **B.** JAR
6. Answer **D.** Has to request access
7. Answer **B.** User has to create response to attack

Chapter 8: Azure Sentinel

Here are some sample answers to the questions presented in this chapter:

1. Answer **C. Security Information Event Management (SIEM)**
2. Answer **C.** A Log Analytics workspace
3. Answer **C.** A variety of data connectors from different vendors
4. Answer **C.** Kusto
5. Answer **A.** Visual detection of issues
6. Answer **B.** Constant monitoring
7. Answer **C.** Analyzing data with Jupyter Notebook

Chapter 9: Security Best Practices

Here are some sample answers to the questions presented in this chapter:

1.   Answer **B.** Use regional workspaces

2.   Answer **B.** Firewall

3.   Answer **D.** All of the above

4.   Answer **A.** Access restriction

5.   Answer **B.** Managed identity

6.   Answer **D.** All of the above

7.   Answer **C.** Different services and features

Other Books You May Enjoy

If you enjoyed this book, you may be interested in these other books by Packt:

Azure Networking Cookbook

Mustafa Toroman

ISBN: 978-1-7898-002-27

- Learn to create Azure networking services
- Understand how to create and work on hybrid connections
- Configure and manage Azure network services
- Learn ways to design high availability network solutions in Azure
- Discover how to monitor and troubleshoot Azure network resources
- Learn different methods of connecting local networks to Azure virtual networks

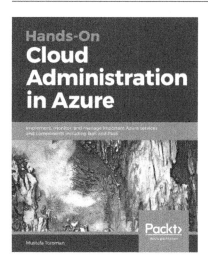

Hands-On Cloud Administration in Azure

Mustafa Toroman

ISBN: 978-1-78913-496-4

- Understand the concepts of IaaS and PaaS
- Learn design patterns for Azure solutions
- Design data solutions in Azure
- Explore concepts of hybrid clouds with Azure
- Implement Azure Security in cloud
- Create and manage Azure resources with script-based tools

Leave a review - let other readers know what you think

Please share your thoughts on this book with others by leaving a review on the site that you bought it from. If you purchased the book from Amazon, please leave us an honest review on this book's Amazon page. This is vital so that other potential readers can see and use your unbiased opinion to make purchasing decisions, we can understand what our customers think about our products, and our authors can see your feedback on the title that they have worked with Packt to create. It will only take a few minutes of your time, but is valuable to other potential customers, our authors, and Packt. Thank you!

Index

deployment models 19
dictionary attacks 50-52
Discover resources 88
Distributed Denial of Service (DDoS) 10
Dynamic Data Masking 158

E

elliptic curve (EC) 128
enable phone sign-in 93
enterprise agreement (EA) 24
Enterprise Mobility + Security (EMS) 95

F

Fabric Controller (FC) 12
FIDO2 security key 94
Firewall settings
  options 216

G

General Data Protection
    Regulation (GDPR) 158
generally available (GA) 174
governance
  in Azure 18, 19
  management groups, using for 23-27
  reference link 18

H

hardware security module
    (HSM) 128, 151
Hybrid authentication 89-92
Hypertext Transfer Protocol over Secure
    Socket Layer (HTTPS) 147

I

identity-focused attack 49
incoming network traffic (ingress) 214
Infrastructure as a Service (IaaS) 5, 153
Infrastructure as Code (IaC) 214
Internet Service Providers (ISPs) 10

J

JSON Web Key (JWK) 128
Just In Time (JIT)
  about 188
  VM, accessing 188-190

K

Key Performance Indicators (KPIs) 200
key vault secret
  referencing, in ARM templates 142-144
  referencing, in Terraform 141, 142
Kusto Query Language (KQL) 40

L

licensing considerations 95
linked template 143
Local Network Gateway (LNG) 110

M

managed identities
  for Azure Resources 133-136
  system-assigned managed identity 133
  user-assigned managed identity 133
Managed Identity (MI) 38
management groups
  using, for governance 23-27

V

virtual machine (VM) 5, 82, 152, 214
Virtual Network Gateway (VNG) 109
virtual networks
  security, considering 119
virtual private networks (VPNs) 74
VNet
  connecting, to another VNet 113-115
  service endpoints 116-118

W

Web Application Firewall (WAF) 123
workbooks
  creating 206-209

Made in the USA
Middletown, DE
20 October 2020